Getting Over It!
Why Korea Needs to
Stop Bashing Japan
by
Sonfa Oh

Translated
by
Ichiro Otani

Tachibana Publishing

First Edition: First Impression July 31, 2015

Published by Tachibana Publishing
Tachibana Shuppan Bldg.
2-20-9 Nishiogi-minami
Suginami-ku Tokyo 167-0053, Japan
Tel. 81-3-5941-2341
Fax. 81-3-5941-2348

Book and Cover Design Shigeo Kawakami

Printed in Japan

Contents

Getting Over It!

Why Korea Needs to Stop Bashing Japan

Getting Over It!
Why Korea Needs to
Stop Bashing Japan

This book is a translation of *Naze hannichi Kankoku ni mirai wa nai no ka*, which was published by Shogakukan Inc. in December 2013

Preface

This book, *Getting Over it! Why Korea Needs to Stop Bashing Japan*, is an English edition of my Japanese book *Naze hannichi Kankoku ni mirai wa nai no ka* [*Why the Anti-Japan Korea Has No Future*], which was published by a Japanese publishing company, Shogakukan, in late 2013.

The relationship between Japan and South Korea continued to deteriorate in 2014. During my lectures and discussion sessions in the past two years, many listeners and participants asked me if there was an English edition of the aforementioned Japanese book. Unfortunately, at that time, there was no English edition of the book; in fact, I knew of no books written in English that shed light on details of the historical facts concerning the Japan-Korea relationship.

In the spring of 2014, a Japanese man living in the United States happened to read the Japanese book. He is Mr. Ichiro Otani, who used to work at the International Monetary Fund for more than 30 years and is currently teaching at the Graduate School of International Public Policy at Hitotsubashi University in Tokyo. Later in the year, he told the editor of the book, Mr. Koichi Sato of the Shogakukan publishing company, that he learned a lot of historical details about the Japan-Korea relations and that it would be useful if an English edition of the book were made available to readers in English-speaking countries and regions. So he suggested to the editor that he ask me if I would be interested in having my book's English edition published. Of course, I answered affirmatively. Without Mr. Otani's suggestion and translation of the book, its English edition would not have been published, and I would like to express my sincere appreciation for his translation and encouragement.

I would also like to express my heartfelt gratitude to Mr. Haruhisa Handa, president of Tachibana Publishing Inc. for his guidance and support in publishing the English edition. President Handa is the founder of the International Academy of Shinto and is also an entrepreneur managing more than ten companies in Japan and abroad. At the same time, he is very active in the fields of opera, paintings, calligraphy, theater, Noh, and philanthropy in Japan. President Handa, with his love for Japan, agreed to publish the English edition of my book.

Last but not least, I would like to thank Mr. Yoshinobu Miyake, managing director of the International Academy of Shinto, who introduced me to President Handa, and Mr. Koichi Sato of the Shogakukan publishing company for their support.

I sincerely hope that this book will help world citizens deepen their understanding of historical facts regarding Japan-Korea relations and contribute to improving these relations.

Sonfa Oh
May 2015

Preface by Translator

When I was visiting Tokyo in the spring of 2014, I saw the Japanese version of this book *Naze han-niti Kankoku ni mirai wa nai no ka* (Shogakukan) at a bookstore. Upon purchasing the book, I immediately began to read it and learned a lot about historical details that I had not known before. I thought that many people in the world, particularly those in the English-speaking regions, would benefit from reading this book. I hope that readers will learn to delineate historical facts from fiction.

Relations between South Korea and Japan have deteriorated considerably in recent years, and this deterioration seems to be partly attributable to people's misunderstanding of historical facts or to their believing in distorted or fabricated events.

Regarding the Japan–South Korea relationship, leaders and the mass media in South Korea, as well as its general public, have been insisting that it is crucially important for Japanese to understand the history correctly. That's true. The assertion, however, should apply not only to Japanese, but also to other people all over the world, including Koreans. With this in mind, I asked the author of the book through its editor if she was interested in publishing an English edition of the book. Her reply was affirmative.

Ichiro Otani
February 2015
Potomac, Maryland, U.S.

Introduction

Relations between Japan and South Korea have grown increasingly tense in recent years. President Lee Myung-bak's visit to a disputed island (known as Dokdo in Korea, Takeshima in Japan) in August 2012, near the end of his tenure, was unprecedented and highly acrimonious. Four days later, he called for the Japanese emperor to apologize for Japan's past deeds since its annexation of Korea, a statement that was well received in Korea but generated a strong negative reaction in Japan.

Ties between these two neighbors—both allies of the United States—have been further strained since Park Guen-hye became president in February 2013. In a departure from patterns established by her predecessors, she announced an aggressive anti-Japan policy on the very first day of her presidency.

Park Guen-hye kept with tradition in turning to the United States as her country's most important foreign policy partner. She visited the United States for four days in May 2013 and met with President Barack Obama in Washington, D.C. In an address to the U.S. Congress she implicitly criticized Japan, saying, "Those who are blind to the past cannot see the future," and declared her anti-Japanese stance. Such a declaration in an international forum was highly unusual. Park's predecessors all visited Japan after first traveling to the United States, but Park chose to go to China instead. In June 2013, she met with President Xi Jinping in Beijing, where she aired her complaints about "past history," with Japan in mind. She repeated anti-Japan statements in public, and anti-Japanese sentiment flared up.

When Japan faced Korea in the final game of the East Asian Cup soccer tournament in July 2013, Korean fans hoisted a large banner saying, "People Who Forget History Have No Future." This caused quite a stir. Some people in South Korea thought the fans went too far.

A variety of political and social factors have contributed to the deterioration of the relationship between Japan and South Korea. Since the end of World War II, South Korea's presidents—military and civilian—had espoused the view that their country should base its relationship with Japan on a future-oriented strategy that does not dwell on the past. But in the course of their tenure, each became more aggressive toward Japan. In each case, as the president faced various crises and flagging popular support, he attempted to deflect the attention of the general public away from domestic problems by invoking the issue of a "foreign enemy," namely Japan.

Anti-Japan ideology in South Korea has evolved over the years. The public has changed its arguments to suit its needs and circumstances at different times. Rhee Syng-man established South Korea's first military government in 1948, three years after the end of World War II. Park Chung-hee and others maintained a military regime. Kim Young-sam established a civilian government in 1993. Kim Tae-jung, Roh Moo-hyun, and Lee Myung-bak all maintained civilian governments.

It is only in recent years that statements like "Japan has no future" have become a public mantra. It is not clear whether such statements are related to my book, *There Is No Future for Anti-Japan Korea*, which I first published in Japanese in 2001 (Shogakukan Bunko). At the time of publication, I was harshly treated in the South Korean mass media. The expression "There is no future" made South Koreans very angry, as evidenced by opinions expressed in newspapers and Internet blogs. If the expression "There is no future for Japan" was triggered by my book, that would indeed be very regrettable.

In writing about anti-Japan ideology in South Korea, I have often thought that Japan is not well understood.

This book (***Getting Over It! Why Korea Needs to Stop Bashing Japan***) argues that the narrow egoism and prejudice of the anti-Japan view reflects Korea's history and its racial characteristics. The backbone of South Korea's anti-Japan ideology is a capricious and opportunistic egoism aimed at satisfying its cliquish mentality, for which Korean leaders often resorted to fabrication of historical events. Such ideology eats away South Korea from within. If South Korea continues this way, South Korean society will collapse. That is why I believe that anti-Japan Korea has no future.

Unless South Korea revises the thinking that has led to the present situation, and its leaders look at the historical facts squarely and clear of distorted and fabricated historical events, it will have no bright future. The main purpose of this book is to document historical facts and to suggest how Japan should deal with South Korea.

Sonfa Oh
May 2015

Chapter I

Raging Anti-Japan Storm in Park Guen-hye's South Korea

Unprecedented, aggressive anti-Japan policy

S outh Korea's stance toward Japan changed radically in 2013, which will be remembered as an epoch-making year of great historic significance.

As soon as Shinzo Abe was elected prime minister for his second term on December 26, 2012, newspapers in South Korea bruited about that "an extreme right-wing government" was established.

Park Guen-hye was elected president of South Korea at almost exactly the same time, on December 19, 2012, and right away launched into her foreign policy of slighting Japan and attaching greater importance to China. She took office on February 25, 2013, and repeated her anti-Japan rhetoric whenever she could. Since then, her anti-Japan stance has been picked up, not only by the government, but also by opposition parties, mass media, the legal community, and the rest of the private sector. Even UN Secretary–General Ban Ki-moon, a former South Korean diplomat, gave strong support to Park's anti-Japan posture. From the spring of 2013, newspapers vigorously started criticizing

Japan, accusing it of "potentially restoring militarism."

It was unprecedented for a South Korean government to take such a strident anti-Japan stance right from the outset. Since the establishment of civilian government in 1993, Seoul has maintained a consistent message on three issues that are bones of contention with Tokyo—"understanding history," "Takeshima (Dok-do)," and "Yasukuni Shrine." But past governments were never so bitter in their criticism of Japan, particularly not early in their tenure; instead, they all adopted a moderate tone and a forward orientation. Anti-Japan rhetoric had been a tool that South Korean governments employed as time wore on and their public support waned. This shift usually took place a few years after each president came to power.

It was August 2011, the fourth year of Lee Myung-bak's presidency, when his policy toward Japan became antagonistic. This reached a peak in August 2012, due to two unprecedented events: President Lee visited the remote island of Takeshima (Dok-do), which is claimed by both South Korea and Japan, and he demanded that Japan's emperor apologize for the country's actions during the period since its annexation of Korea. Since then, Japan-Korea relations have deteriorated rapidly.

The Japanese government hoped strongly that Park Guen-hye would help patch up the poor relationship between the two countries. But that was not to be.

I was barred from entering South Korea

My own experience in being barred from entering South Korea illustrates the unusual nature of the Park Guen-hye government's policy toward Japan.

Ever since I became a reviewer in 1990, the press in South Korea has been critical of my views. Under three governments, headed by Roh Tae-woo, Kim Young-sam, and Kim Tae-jung, I have been indirectly subjected to various unpleasant incidents, but I had never been subjected to the government's direct interference until 2007.

On October 1, 2007, the South Korean government barred me from entering the country. This incident took place after I became a naturalized Japanese citizen. On that day in October, I was to visit Jeju-do for my mother's funeral, but I was stopped at the airport. No airport personnel explained to me the reasons; the only thing they said, repeatedly, was "orders from superiors."

I made telephone calls to my Japanese acquaintances, who in turn sought assistance from the Japanese consulate and the Japanese embassy. After being held at the airport for many hours, I was finally allowed to enter South Korea and attend the funeral, on the condition that I would "not engage in anti–South Korea activities, and leave the country immediately after the funeral."

Throughout the administration of President Lee Myung-bak, I was able to travel freely between South Korea and Japan. Even after Park Guen-hye took office, I had no difficulty entering South Korea in April 2013 or May 2013. However, on July 27 of that year, when I arrived at the Inchon Airport to attend my niece's wedding, I was again denied entry.

Once again, no one told me the reasons. As before, I contacted Japanese friends and asked them to get assistance from the Japanese embassy or the Japanese Ministry of Foreign Affairs. This time, however, it was a Saturday. It was difficult to contact these agencies. In the end, the South Korean authorities deported me to Japan.

I was put on a flight bound for Narita Airport. A flight attendant took my passport to hold it during the flight. Upon arrival at Narita, the flight attendant handed over an envelope to a woman—perhaps an official from the Ministry of Justice—who opened it and gave my passport back to me. The envelope also contained a document concerning the deportation order from South Korea's Ministry of Justice. It stated, "According to Article 76 of the Immigration Management Law, the person identified below is ordered to be deported from the Republic of Korea with your government bearing the cost of transportation."

South Korea's Immigration Management Law (Article 11, and Article 76, Paragraph 2) says exactly who is prohibited from entering South Korea. Article 11 states that people who carry contagious diseases or who have psychiatric illness may not enter. In addition, according to Paragraph 3, "people who have been identified by the government as individuals having reasonable risks for possible action that is detrimental to the country's benefits and public security." Although they never said so explicitly, I am quite sure this is why the authorities stopped me from entering South Korea.

In late April 2013 I had a dinner meeting with Prime Minister Shinzo Abe. This prompted the South Korean newspaper *Chosun Ilbo* (April 29, 2013) to criticize me, under the headline "Dinner Meeting with Anti–South Korea Extreme Right Wing." This article came at a time when the South Korean government was repeatedly expressing its anti-Japan posture and criticism against the Abe government. I believe it was this incident that prompted the South Korean government to put me back on the blacklist of people barred from entering South Korea.

It is clear to me that the reasons for keeping me out of South Korea were my criticism of South Korea and statements I made regarding the period of Japanese rule over Korea. Such a ban is a blatant infringement of human rights, freedom of speech, and freedom of movement. South Korea's mass media reported widely on the government's action of barring my entry into South Korea. The following excerpt is typical.

"Ms. Sonfa Oh, a South Korean–born Japanese, infamous for her slandering and defaming South Korea, was denied entry into South Korea. Many people applauded the government action. As a reporter, I felt good about it also…. I feel that we should show our indignation to Japanese right-wing groups, which freely did whatever they wanted to do against South Korea." (*Chosun Ilbo*, August 2, 2013)

I can easily imagine that Internet bloggers or Anti-Japan Nationalist Groups might criticize me, using offensive and emotional language, but it is hard to understand how a major newspaper could do this. That sort of thing has never happened before. It was also a big surprise that no South Korean media aired even the slightest opposing views based on freedom of speech and human rights.

Park Guen-hye clings to anti-Japan stance

Many major Japanese press outlets expressed the hope that President Park Guen-hye would have "favorable views toward Japan" and that "Korea-Japan relations would improve." But such hopes have always been a mystery to me. It has been clear all along that Park Guen-hye has remained consistent in her anti-Japan policies. Her stance has been clear since she decided to run for the presidency.

Some examples:

When Park Guen-hye visited Japan, a reporter asked her, "The Dok-do problem is complicated. Do you have a plan to solve it?" She replied, "Dok-do is South Korean territory. The problem can be easily solved if Japan accepts this." President Park said she has been encouraging Japan to embrace a correct understanding of history (press interview on August 20, 2012, after she officially became the Saenuri Party candidate for president).

"If Japan does not give up its argument that Dok-do is Japanese territory, economic cooperation, security cooperation, and cultural exchanges will be hindered in future generations, and we will lose a lot" (interview with South Korean press, September 14, 2012).

"Unless Japan makes concessions, there will be a great impact on the relation between the two countries" (ibid).

"Dok-do is solely South Korea's territory in the light of history, geography, and international laws."

"To make progress in the two countries' relations, Japan must look at this point seriously."

"('Comfort women issues') cannot be rationalized under any circumstances. Japan and South Korea share the value of democracy and human rights. Therefore, I hope wise leaders of Japan would carefully take into account these views."

(Interview with a foreign correspondent in Seoul, November 8, 2012)

"[For the sake of improving South Korea-Japan relations], it is necessary for Japan to hold the correct understanding of the history."

(Presidential candidates debate on TV, December 4, 2012)

Within a few days after taking office as president, Park Guen-hye made the following remarks.

"Japan must look at history directly, and must positively pursue changes and act responsibly."

"When Japan reflects honestly on history, the opportunity for co-prosperity will open up in the future."

"The historical situation facing the aggressors and their victims will never change even if 1,000 years pass."

"(Japan and South Korea) must correctly understand the history and act responsibly. Only then will trust emerge between the two countries."

(Government ceremony commemorating Independence Movements, March 1, 2013)

On March 11, 2013, the government of South Korea was invited to a memorial service for victims of the Great East Japan

Earthquake of 2011. South Korean ambassador to Japan Shin Gak-su refused to attend. The following day, he explained, "Due to administrative mistakes, I did not know about the Japanese government's invitation and could not attend the memorial service." He did not utter one word of apology. The South Korean government is obviously following in the footsteps of China, which refused to attend the service as a protest against the Japanese government, because Tokyo had asked the government of Taiwan to offer flowers at the memorial service. This would appear to indicate that the Park Guen-hye government doesn't think we can hope for the emergence of mutual trust.

President Park Guen-hye is to blame for the bad relationship between South Korea and Japan

In 2013, Japan–South Korea relations deteriorated to their worst state since normalization in 1965. The facts show clearly that it is President Park Guen-hye who is responsible for this situation.

Prime Minister Abe regarded the building of friendly relations with South Korea to be the most important issue for his government, particularly in view of the escalating dispute between Japan and China over the Senkaku Islands and North Korea's implementation of nuclear tests. As soon as he and Park Guen-hye were elected to the highest office in their respective nations, Abe enthusiastically took initiatives to improve relations with South Korea. Park, however, took an antithetical stance, continuously espousing her antipathy to Japan.

On December 16, 2012, the Liberal Democratic Party of Japan won a landslide victory in the general election for the Lower House of the national legislature, known as the Diet, making it clear that Abe would be the next prime minister. On December 19, it was confirmed that Park Guen-hye had won the presidential election in South Korea. The following day, Abe told reporters, "I would like to communicate with South Korea's new president closely, and I want to deepen the Japan–South Korea relationship, taking a broad view of the situation." Since that day, Mr. Abe and his government have publicly stated the following:

2012:

- December 21: The government postponed its scheduled "Takeshima ceremony" that Abe publicly promised during the election campaign to hold. Japan decided to dispatch a special envoy to the new president of South Korea.
- December 23: Abe announced his intention to postpone his visit to the Yasukuni Shrine during its Spring Festival.
- December 27: The chief cabinet secretary stated the government will abide by former Prime Minister Tomiichi Murayama's statement of apology.

2013:

- January 1: Prime Minister Abe said, "South Korea shares with Japan the values of democracy and a market-based economic system, and is the most important neighboring country."
- January 4: Prime Minister Abe sent Diet member Fukushiro Nukaga as his special envoy to South Korea. Nukaga handed

president-elect Park Guen-hye a personal letter from Abe, in which he stated that South Korea is "the most important neighboring country."

- January 9: The Ministry of Foreign Affairs publicly announced that, for the time being, Japan will not make a unilateral presentation to the International Court of Justice on the territorial issue related to Takeshima.

- February 25: Deputy Prime Minister Taro Aso paid a courtesy call on Park Guen-hye at her inauguration. He emphasized the Japanese government's policy of regarding South Korea with great importance, noting that South Korea is the most important neighboring country, sharing with Japan the values of democracy and the rule of law, etc.

- May 7: The Japanese Cabinet issued a statement that the government would adhere to Kono's statement of apology.

- June 1: Defense Minister Itsunori Onodera severely criticized Osaka Mayor Toru Hashimoto for making inappropriate remarks regarding comfort women during World War II. "Hashimoto repeatedly made inappropriate remarks regarding Japan's past history and led to neighboring countries' misunderstanding and mistrust."

- August 15: Prime minister postponed his visit to Yasukuni Shrine.

As these facts show, the Japanese government has attached great importance to South Korea from the very beginning of Park's presidency, more than ever before.

What about President Park's behavior?

On December 19, 2012, the day after her victory at the polls, the president-elect met with ambassadors from various countries. In a break from tradition, she met the ambassador from China before she saw the ambassador from Japan. In addition, Park announced her intention to send her first special envoy to China, but she remained silent about whether she would send an envoy to Japan. When Abe announced his intention to send a special envoy to South Korea, Park refused to receive the envoy, saying there had been no prior discussion, and she did not know of the Japanese government's plan.

South Korea's main policies toward Japan, as evidenced by the president, the government, the legal community, and the private sector, are shown below.

2013:

- January 3: Seoul High Court decided the South Korean government should refuse Japanese authorities' request for the extradition to Japan of a Chinese national, accused of setting a fire on the premises of Yasukuni Shrine, imprisoned in South Korea.

- February 26: Daejun District Court made a provisional ruling that the South Korean government should stop the repatriation to Japan of one of two statues that were stolen from a temple and a shrine in Tsushima City, Nagasaki Prefecture.

- March 1: President Park remarked at a government ceremony remembering the Independence Movement that "The historical situation facing the assailants and their victims will never change even if 1,000 years pass."

- March 11: The South Korean government ignored the Japanese government's invitation to memorial services for victims of the Great East Japan Earthquake.

- May 3: South Korea and China did not attend the ASEAN+3 meeting of finance ministers and central bank governors.

- May 7: During a U.S.–South Korea summit meeting in Washington, D.C., President Park said, "For the maintenance of peace in Northeast Asia, Japan must understand the correct history." In an interview with a *Washington Post* reporter, she said Japan should look into a mirror and have a responsible understanding of history.

- May 8: In a speech to the U.S. Congress, President Park said, with Japan in mind, that "those who are blind to history have no future."

- June 27-30: President Park became the first president to visit China before visiting Japan. A joint communiqué issued at the end of the summit stated, with Japan in mind, that disputes and mistrust among the countries in the region have deepened due to recent history and problems triggered by this history.

- July 3: A South Korean private organization made a presentation to the International Olympic Committee (IOC) saying that Tokyo was not qualified to host the Summer Olympic Games in 2020.

- July 10: Seoul High Court ruled that Nippon Steel & Sumitomo Metal Corp. (formed through the 2012 merger of Nippon Steel and Sumitomo Metal Co.) should pay compensation to four deceased South Korean employees who were forced to work at the company in the immediate aftermath of World War II.

- July 30: Busan High Court handed a similar decision to Mitsubishi Heavy Industry Co.

- August 26: At a news conference in Seoul, UN Secretary General Ban Ki-moon made the unusual statement that Japan's government and political leaders must reflect deeply on themselves, and must have an international- and future-oriented vision.

- September 6: The South Korean government banned imports from eight Japanese prefectures, including Fukushima, Tochigi, and Gunma.

- September 6: In a meeting with the German chancellor, President Park said Japan had rubbed salt on the wounds of history instead of making efforts to heal them. She said Japan's attitude would not help resolve the difficult issues between the two countries and that she hopes Japan would face history correctly and be able to construct a future-oriented relationship between the two countries.

- September 17: It was revealed that the South Korean government had expressed its opposition to the Japanese government's efforts for the inclusion on UNESCO's World Heritage List of sites in Kyushu, Yamaguchi, and elsewhere, as part of Japan's Industrial Revolution heritage during the Meiji era.

From developments such as these, it is clear that President Park, as the leader of South Korea, has been the main culprit in the deterioration of the Japan–South Korea relationship, while

Japan has continued to promote a friendly relationship with South Korea.

Honor student of South Korea's anti-Japan education

Why have many Japanese journalists held high hopes for Park Guen-hye? As far as I can tell, it is merely because she is the daughter of former president Park Chung-hee. That is the only reason.

Park Chung-hee was certainly pro-Japanese as a private citizen, but as a public figure he pushed an anti-Japan policy. Park Chung-hee, like Rhee Syng-man before him, thought that anti-communist and anti-Japan policies were the only option to bring together South Korea as one nation.

During the period of Park Chung-hee's government (1963–1979), I was in school in South Korea: primary school, middle school, and then high school. At that time, it was the norm in South Korea to refer to Japanese people with derogatory expressions such as *oenom* or *jokpari* (an expression that compares a foot wearing a split-toed Japanese sock to a pig's hoof). In those days, we were constantly told that Japanese people had harmed our ancestors and were cold-blooded and devilish. Most people who are now about 60 years old or younger have internalized strong anti-Japanese feelings, because the education they received was strongly biased against Japan. But many older people, who did not receive postwar education, have positive memories of Japanese rule. The current situation is greatly influenced by when people received their education.

In 2013, Park Guen-hye was 61 years old. Like others in her age cohort, she belongs to the generation that received anti-Japan education under the Park Chung-hee regime. Even if Park Chung-hee may have been pro-Japan as a private citizen, he could never have told his daughter that what was written in her textbooks was a lie. The same was true at my home. Parents who used to work in Japan during Japanese rule often expressed favorable views of the Japanese. My parents just listened quietly when I told them about "imperial Japan's atrocious acts" that I learned about at school. I heard that in Taiwan some parents told their children that what was written in their textbooks were lies, but I never heard of any such thing in South Korea.

Judging from President Park Guen-hye's remarks in the past, it is clear she does not share some of the basic knowledge about Japan that many ordinary South Koreans possess. We often hear on TV that she thinks the territorial issue surrounding Takeshima (Dok-do) can be quickly resolved once Japan abandons its claim. We also hear her repeat that she hopes Japanese intellectuals will come around to the correct understanding of history. In Japan, many people think Park Guen-hye needs to make such remarks for domestic reasons, but that is not necessarily the case. Park Guen-hye, like myself, had it drummed into her at school that Japanese understanding of history is not correct. Until that situation is rectified, there is no hope for good relations between the two countries. She and I both belong to the generation with the strongest anti-Japan views.

First break from tradition

Park Guen-hye's first election to public office was in 1998, when she became a member of the National Assembly at the age of 46. Soon thereafter, she became deputy president of the Saenuri Party. As soon as she entered politics, she quickly established herself as a potential presidential candidate. In June 2000, South Korea and North Korea held a summit meeting, and an atmosphere of affinity with the North spread throughout South Korea. In 1974, a North Korean who had grown up in Japan tried to assassinate Park Chung-hee and killed Park Guen-hye's mother, Yuk Young-su, instead. The assassin was acting under orders from North Korea. It would be understandable for Park Guen-hye to revile North Korea for the rest of her life. But that would have put her out of step with the prevailing political climate and destroyed her chances of winning the presidency.

In 2002, Park Guen-hye visited North Korea and met one-on-one with Kim Jong-il. According to press reports, Kim Jong-il broached the subject of the assassination of Yuk Young-su. He said the terrorist act had been carried out without his knowledge, but he apologized for North Korea's involvement. Park Guen-hye greatly valued this apology and extended an olive branch by saying, "Both of us are of the second generation. Let us try hard." Since the summit meeting between North and South Korea in 2000, public opinion in South Korea has moved firmly in the direction of rapprochement with the North. Like many other politicians, Park Guen-hye calculated her position carefully, putting politics first and telling the public she, too, was pro–North Korea.

This was her first departure from tradition. In Japan, past grudges are often washed away as if by water, but in South Korea this was a politician's careful calculation based on the prevailing mood of the time.

Second break from tradition

In preparing to run for the presidency in 2012, Park Guen-hye had to decide what view to put forward regarding her father's military government. Until that point, she had maintained a positive view of her father's performance, saying publicly that her father's 1961 coup and the resulting "restoration system" (military dictatorship) were necessary to save the country.

The Saenuri Party conditioned its support for her candidacy, however, on a change in her view of her father's military regime. The party thought it not possible to win the election unless she changed her view, and in the end, she gave in to the party's demand.

When she announced her candidacy for president, Park Guen-hye changed her position on the military dictatorship and related incidents. She said the military coup that brought her father to power, the "restoration movement," and the "People's Revolution Party incident" (in which eight people were executed for the crime of instigating disturbances) were not in line with the values of the constitution. She said they had delayed the political development of the Republic of South Korea. "I again apologize to the people and families who suffered from these incidents. I know the pain of losing a family member, and how intense such pain is," she said (press interview, September 24, 2012). On the October 26 anniversary of her father's death, at the memorial service at the National Cemetery, she said, "I would like to sincerely apologize to those people who suffered because of my father's power politics."

By describing the political regime based on military dictatorship led by her own father as a crime, she sought to close that chapter and mark a new start for her own political career with an image as "a daughter of the president who was pure, lived a simple life, with an unprecedentedly clean history, who showed strong leadership, and achieved rapid economic growth."

The focal issues of the presidential election were the correction of income inequality—"economic democratization"—and the elimination of corruption and malfeasance. In the view of the general public, the next president should be a clean and democratic person in whom South Korea could entrust its expectations for economic policy implementation. Park Guen-hye denounced the undemocratic aspects of her father's political regime while echoing his excellent political influence and strong leadership. This posture represented nothing but her opportunistic attitude, but this is the image she strove to put forward in the presidential election campaign.

Not one of South Korea's ten presidents has completed his full term without a hitch or lived a full life after leaving the presidency. Eight of the ten presidents including the last, Lee Myung-bak, experienced exile, imprisonment, assassination, suicide, or a sudden downfall. The last six, from Chun Doo-hwan through Lee

Myung-bak, were arrested or convicted on charges ranging from bribery to profiting from their office and tax evasion. However, President Park Chung-hee, his wife, and his relatives have never been accused of wrongdoing. Park Chung-hee's private life was simple, and he left no significant assets. These aspects of his life have contributed to his great reputation to this day.

"South Korea's princess"

In the eyes of the South Korean public, Park Guen-hye's image is strongly identified with her mother's physical appearance and manner. Her mother, Yuk Young-su, was one of the most admired women in South Korean history. The South Korean media often profess to see in President Park Guen-hye "her father's strong leadership" and "leadership based on her mother's gentle manners."

During Park Chung-hee's presidency, short newsreels that ran in theaters before feature films invariably opened with the national flag and the national anthem. We in the audience would all stand up with our right hands over our hearts. Then, the announcer would say, "Today, President and Madam Park…" Madam Yuk Young-su was always at the president's side, wearing Korea's traditional dress, *chima jeogori*, with her hair braided in back. The president was called "the Nation's Father" and his wife "the Nation's Mother."

The same went for TV news. Every day there was a report, "Today, His Excellency President Park and Madam Park…" This was a pattern that lasted for 16 years. From the day of the May 16 military coup, we were repeatedly taught about the "Difficult Road to the Restoration of Our Homeland." As soon as we saw their picture, we would be flooded with emotion, and tears would flow from our eyes. Unaware, we had become nationalists. Most people now aged 50 and older must have experienced such emotional upwellings in those days.

After the assassination of Yuk Young-su in the middle of Park Chung-hee's presidency, her daughter, Park Guen-hye, carried on in her role as First Lady for the remainder of his term, standing at the president's side. She very closely resembled her mother. From early childhood, she, like her mother, braided her hair in back. She never changed her hairstyle even after becoming a politician. Naturally, her image would echo her mother's. While her father was in office, the South Korean public, including myself, thought of her as the princess of South Korea. She was the daughter of the Nation's Father, thrust into the role of the Nation's Mother. As she grew older, her resemblance to her mother grew ever stronger. When the presidential campaign was in full swing, she was often described as an incarnation of her mother, and she received strong support from her mother's generation.

Tremendous impact of "noble blood lineage"

On the Korean Peninsula, there is a deep-rooted, longstanding tradition of respect for noble bloodlines. In Park Guen-hye's case, though, it is not because she is the second generation of a political family. She is the politician with the noblest blood lineage in postwar South Korea. Park Guen-hye's popularity in South Korea increased tremendously when Kim Jong-un, a grandson of Kim Il-song, succeeded his father Kim Jong-il in North Korea. People in South Korea had become fed up with elite leaders of civilian governments who were accused of corruption one after the next. They rapidly raised their hopes for Park Guen-hye because they thought she would rival Kim Jong-un in terms of prestigious bloodline.

People in South Korea often say North Korea's power-based political regime is not suited to their country, but in fact they would understand the system prevailing in North Korea very well. Heritage, dictatorship, and ignoring poverty (in North Korea) are to be criticized. However, many South Koreans envy North Korea's social and political order under strong management. Leadership in North Korea was handed down from one generation to the next within the same family. The great Nation's Father, Kim Il-sung, was followed by his son, Kim Jong-il, and his grandson, Kim Jong-un. Kim Jong-un's hairstyle, his posture, the way he claps his hands, and his voice all closely resemble his grandfather's. As long as people accept this type of noble blood lineage, the common illusion of the great Nation's Father, the leader's behavior, dictated by genetics, emanates an absolutely effective impact. The impact of Park Guen-hye is basically the same as that of the Kim family leaders of North Korea.

In Asia, it is not unusual for the daughter of an ex-president or an ex-prime minister to succeed her father as head of government. Examples include Indira Gandhi in India, Gloria Macapagal-Arroyo in the Philippines, and Benazir Bhutto in Pakistan. Throughout Asia—with the notable exception of Japan after the Muromachi Period (1392–1573)—farming villages were established on the basis of blood lineage. In South Korea and throughout the rest of Asia, even now, "blood is thicker than water."

Memory of the "Han-gang Miracle" led by her father

When Park Chung-hee was in power, South Korea accomplished rapid economic development in what is called the "Han-gang Miracle." The legacy of her father's "Han-gang Miracle" was one of the main factors contributing to Park Guen-hye's electoral victory. She ended her inauguration speech with the following statement: "Let us, the people, recreate the Han-gang Miracle, and become the main characters in this miracle. Let us make efforts jointly together with others, and create a new period full of happiness and hope for the people" (inauguration speech, February 25, 2013).

Park Chung-hee had this to say about his economic policies that led to the "Han-gang Miracle."

- Restore and maintain the political and economic system for the people, which had been controlled by a small minority of privileged people.
- Transfer to the society of farmers, workers, and ordinary citizens the rights and leadership that had been manipulated by a small minority of the privileged class, and establish a mass

politics, a mass economy, and a mass culture; create a new elite class, members of which would establish themselves in these areas, and lead a forthcoming people's nation. So to speak, establish a new influential class in the coming period (*The Path that South Korean People Must Take*, March 1962, Seoul; Japanese translation, June 1970, Kashima Research Institute Publishing Association).

The centerpiece for this strategy was the establishment of a national economy; that is, liberation from poverty and the establishment of a strong and wealthy nation. In 1965, President Park Chung-hee normalized relations with Japan. He built a foundation for economic development based on massive financial aid and technical assistance from Japan under the Treaty on Basic Relations between Japan and the Republic of South Korea, and he achieved the "Han-gang Miracle," following the model of Japanese economic growth strategy after World War II.

I recall the experiences of my own youth, right in the midst of the Miracle. I realized that the pursuit of one's own interests or advancement in society was identical to working for the good of our nation. I grasped the hope that we could achieve the true union of our people through the gradual accumulation of individual work experiences. I think many people thought the same way.

The "Han-gang Miracle" brought about economic development in leaps and bounds. However, this achievement was fundamentally different from the kind of economic development that has been achieved since the establishment of civilian government in South Korea, or in recent years in China. The middle class expanded, and the gap between rich and poor shrank rapidly, closely resembling the kind of development that took place in Japan in the decade or so after World War II. Looking back, it was a wonderful time. That is why South Koreans had such fervid hope for Park Guen-hye to narrow once again the gap between rich and poor that unfortunately had widened so much under the presidents who followed her father, and to realize economic growth aiming at raising the living standards of the middle class.

A second "Han-gang Miracle" becomes unattainable

Backed by these hopes of the South Korean people, in her inauguration speech Park Guen-hye stressed the importance of achieving the "Second Han-gang Miracle."

- I would like to move forward side by side with you, the proud people of South Korea, to meet the great challenge of establishing a new period full of hope, and the second Han-gang Miracle. I will open a new period, when the great happiness of each of you, the people, will become the scale of the nation's power and the people will share that power.

- When the elements of the economic system converge into one, and every one of you unites, you the people will obtain happiness and raise the competitiveness of our country. I will achieve economic restoration based on such a foundation and achieve the second Han-gang Miracle that would bring happiness to you, the people (inauguration speech, February 25, 2013).

For those who experienced the first Han-gang Miracle, this appeal from the president brought back memories. Parents and educators talked about the Miracle as the "Great Story of the Past." But achieving the first Han-gang Miracle had involved massive amounts of funding and technical assistance from Japan. Park Chung-hee never told the people this. The majority of South Koreans believed at that time—and still do—that the Han-gang Miracle was achieved by South Korea on its own, thanks to the leadership of Park Chung-hee.

- It was because the people had never been told the truth about the first Miracle that Park Guen-hye was able to capitalize on her father's image and campaign by emphasizing the importance of achieving a second Han-gang Miracle. But this has clearly turned out to be no more than wishful thinking. Within a month after Park Guen-hye took office as president, many of her cabinet members and vice ministers had to resign due to charges of corruption, tax evasion, and sexual harassment. The South Korean won continued to appreciate, and with the performance of conglomerates deteriorating, already by the end of 2013 Park Guen-hye's government needed to set aside the original policy of "economic growth aiming at securing employment" and shift to a new policy of protecting large corporations.

Park Guen-hye's government, which had adopted anti-Japan policies from the very beginning, no longer holds the trump card of diverting the people's attention to a foreign enemy. No matter how far her public support fell, that tactic was of no use to her.

When the government faces a crisis due to loss of popular

support, both the bureaucracy and the private sector will abandon it, and President Park's elite bloodline will be of no avail. I fear the South Korean government could be destabilized by a development like this.

I have a good reason for my fear. Both public opinion and official opinion regarding North Korea are now sharply divided in South Korea, and the government is sitting on a delicate balance. The government is stuck in a situation where it can only strive desperately to maintain that balance.

Pro-North elements in South Korea equate nationalism with opposition to Japan

Concerning North Korea, the view of the ruling Saenuri Party (formerly known as the Hannara Party) is that South Korea will not engage in any discussion with North Korea as long as the North insists on continuing nuclear research and nuclear weapons; aid from the South will be kept to the minimum level of humanitarian relief. The largest opposition party, the Democratic Party, advocates reopening the "sunshine policy" of easing relations with Pyongyang, providing aid the way Presidents Kim Tae-jung and Roh Moo-hyun did, and promoting dialogue with North Korea without preconditions.

When Kim Tae-jung and Roh Moo-hyung were in office, Seoul was very interested in improving relations with North Korea, but North Korea's influence waned when Lee Myung-bak became president, for a number of reasons. North Korea resumed its nuclear tests. A South Korean tourist visiting Mount Kumgang in North Korea was shot dead. North Korea attacked a South Korean vessel in the Yellow Sea, and later carried out a torpedo attack against a South Korean warship. Then, North Korean artillery launched an attack against Yeonpyeong-do.

Following these incidents, the South Korean government stopped its dialogue with North Korea. The influence of pro-North elements in South Korea declined, and the current government came to adopt a harsh posture toward North Korea. The strength of the two opposing groups that became rivals was roughly equally matched.

President Park Guen-hye attached great importance to maintaining her predecessor's principles vis-à-vis the North. Her government displayed a strong willingness to respond militarily to North Korean marine attacks and to hold joint military exercises with U.S. forces. Political confrontations regarding a policy toward North Korea led naturally to confrontations regarding economic and social policies. The ruling Saenuri Party and its allies pushed their neoliberal policies, while the opposition parties advocated policies that tended toward democratic socialism.

Shortly after Park Guen-hye took office as president, however, she shifted her position. While her government still wanted Pyongyang to relinquish both nuclear research and nuclear weapons, it would also promote the process of building trust in the peninsula through dialogue and humanitarian assistance. This shift clearly reflected the president's awareness of the source of the opposition parties' influence and her desire to keep her balance on the tightrope. Park Guen-hye's tenuous balance of power is closely related to the high level of anti-Japan sentiment in South Korea.

Under the U.S. military government that followed the Korean War, the U.S. authorities staffed South Korea's administrative systems with civil servants, policemen, military officers, and others who had previously worked under the Japanese colonial rulers. This pattern continued under Rhee Syng-man and under Park Chung-hee. When the Japan-South Korea Normalization Treaty was concluded in 1965, South Korea received a large sum of financial assistance, but the government allocated only a tiny fraction of this money to the people as postwar compensation. Most of it was used to finance industrialization. This led opposition parties to lean toward North Korea (North Korea Loyalists) and brand Park Chung-hee as an unforgivable Japan lackey, and later to use this idea as a stick with which to beat Park Guen-hye.

After the North-South summit meeting between Kim Tae-jung and Kim Jong-il, Pyongyang sympathizers in the South called for "love toward the compatriots," advocating "nationalism" that extended to opposing Japan as a different race. Needless to say, this view equated "pro-Japan" ideas with "treason."

On February 12, 2013, North Korea conducted its third nuclear test, and on March 8 the UN decided to impose sanctions on North Korea. Since that time, North Korea has escalated its aggression, repeating provocation after provocation, even threatening to attack the mainland of the United States. As a result, popular support for pro-North elements in South Korea has waned.

The left-wing influences struggled to recover by emphasizing their anti-Japan posture, hiding their essential nature of sympathizing with the North and even advocating subjugation to Pyongyang. This has helped their cause, and their influence has spread again throughout society. North Korean spies in South Korea are said to number about 120,000. They have infiltrated deep into government institutions, mass media, and other institutions, and they have been drumming up anti-Japan sentiment among the general public.

Pro-North political influences, wearing their "cloak of invisibility" as opponents of Japan, have hammered away at their message that South Korean patriotism equals opposition to Japan. At the same time, the ruling party is also strongly embracing the same equation, to win public support. Thus, nationalism seems the same on the surface on both sides, but there are subtle differences. As long as the government remains steadfast in its opposition to Japan, it can steal support away from pro-North groups, which have also been opposed to Japan from the outset.

This is the essential nature of Park Guen-hye's unusually strong opposition to Japan, which she voiced as soon as she became president.

Chapter II

How South Korea's Anti-Japan Ideology Took Form

South Korea was founded on the idea that anti-Japan equals justice

South Korea's anti-Japan ideology is not simply a political strategy. South Korea as a nation is based on an ideology that equates opposition to Japan with justice. Needless to say, justice for South Korea as a nation is the fundamental rationale that every citizen must believe in. The ideology of opposition to Japan is the main spiritual backbone that holds South Korea together as a nation.

How did opposition to Japan become synonymous with justice in South Korea? In the three years between Japan's defeat in World War II and the founding of the Republic of Korea, a momentous power struggle took place. In the end, elements ideologically opposed to Japan emerged victorious with a firm grip on political power, and they were the ones that founded the nation.

According to the official history, the Republic of Korea (South Korea) is the successor to a provisional government that had been headquartered in Chongqing, China, since pre–World War II. The preamble of South Korea's constitution states: "We, the people of Korea, proud of a resplendent history and traditions dating from time immemorial, upholding the cause of the Provisional Republic of Korea Government born of the March First Independence Movement of 1919...."

This is why South Korea takes opposition to Japan as its fundamental concept of justice. The prewar provisional government was established by a political group whose origins lay in the 3.1 Independence Movement that fought against Japanese colonial rule in 1919. That group included Rhee Syng-man and Kim Gu, who were leaders of the anti-Japan independence movement in exile. The provisional government was established in Shanghai, and a similar provisional government was established in Siberia. Later, the two merged in Shanghai. After the Sino-Japan war began in 1931, the Korean government was evacuated to Chongqing in 1940. Neither the Axis powers nor the Allies, nor any other nations, recognized this Korean government.

The Provisional Government of the Republic of Korea was no more than a group of politicallyengaged Koreans in exile. Its leaders held the group to be the legitimate government of Korea, and that was a dream they were able to realize. That is present-day South Korea. The members of that original group were not active in the Korean territory; they were intellectuals who lived abroad for a long time. Needless to say, they had no influence within the country until later. Nevertheless, these individuals were the core activists who established the nation. It is the deepening cold war between the United States and the Soviet Union that contributed to the creation of the Republic of Korea.

The United States had established military government in

South Korea, keeping pro-Japan elements within the country from returning to power. In the immediate aftermath of the war, the United States did not recognize the legitimacy of the Provisional Government of the Republic of Korea. Nevertheless, they saw Rhee Syng-man as the most pro-U.S. and anti-communist among Korean leaders, and the U.S. supported him wholeheartedly. With this strong backing, Rhee Syng-man was able to sideline his political rivals and consolidate his own leadership position.

A general election was held in South Korea in 1948, and the National Assembly that was established chose Rhee Syng-man as the nation's president. His government promulgated the nation's constitution, and at the same time the "Anti-Race Activities Punishment Law." Under this law, Rhee Syng-man arrested senior government officials who remained loyal to Japan in their hearts, and in effect purged them. This is how pro-Japan groups lost their influence immediately after the establishment of South Korea.

South Korea eventually fabricated a history that the independence movements liberated the nation from the Japanese imperialists, that the nation was freed from Japanese colonial rule by the courageous struggle of the people of South Korea. Through education and propaganda, the government vigorously indoctrinated the people with this fabricated history.

This is how the notion that justice equals opposition to Japan has become the fundamental ideology of South Korea, the idea that Korea's independence was won by independence movements led by the Provisional Government of the Republic of Korea. The fact, however, is that Korea automatically became independent following Japan's defeat by the Allied Powers in World War II. But the emergent government of South Korea held fast to the notion that justice had been achieved as a result of its opposition to Japan, as a means of uniting the public.

Treatment of pro-Japan groups as point of struggle between right and left

Under Rhee Syng-man's government, however, there was widespread recognition of the fact that Korea's independence was an incidental consequence of Japan's defeat by the Allies in World War II, and not the result of Koreans' efforts. Koreans did not have the power to defeat Japan. It was only much later—after the emergence of civilian government—that the myth emerged that Korea's independence was achieved by the courageous independence movements of the Korean people."

On August 15, 1954, Rhee Syng-man himself stated the following during a Liberation Day ceremony: "To tell the truth, we cannot say that today is the true liberation day. It is a fact that only half of our peninsula was liberated, and our friends have protected us from the threat of the Communist Party." (*Collection of President and Dr. Rhee Syng-man Speeches and Conversations* [in Korean], Vol. 2, Office of Public Information, Republic of Korea, 1956)

August 15 is still the day commemorating liberation from Japanese rule and the founding of the nation. However, Rhee Syngman said August 15 brought only partial liberation, and Korea was able to become independent only through the actions of the U.S. military. He did not say that Korea won its independence from Japan.

This is an important point. Rhee Syng-man felt it was proper to regard August 15 as Liberation Day, but it was not proper to regard it as the "Day for Restoring Honor." The people of Korea often refer to August 15 as "Independence Day," rather than Liberation Day.

The treatment of pro-Japan groups was one of the biggest controversies to plague the nation from its inception. "Pro-Japan groups" does not refer to people who simply hold favorable views of Japan or some sort of pro-Japan doctrine. Instead, it refers to people who collaborated in some way with the Japanese colonial administration in Korea. In Korean ideological terms, the founding of the nation should have been accomplished without the support of pro-Japan elements. As a practical matter, however, such elements were necessary, because they were the Koreans who had the knowledge and experience of how to govern.

In fact, almost all of the senior staff members of the Rhee Syng-man government were people who worked in the government institutions of the Japanese colonial administration of Korea, known as the Government-General of Korea, and who cooperated directly or indirectly with that administration's economic and social policies. In the immediate aftermath of World War II, Korean officials who had worked under the Government-General of Korea continued to work under the U.S. military government in positions of high responsibility for social and economic policy. Other than these people, there were few if any Koreans who could immediately carry out the management of the postwar nation.

The ideological confrontation that arose in this period pitted conservatives against progressives. The main conservative forces were Rhee Syng-man and the Korea Democratic Party, which embraced the idea of excluding pro-Japan groups from the management of the nation. They argued that South Korea needed to shake off the influence of Japan and its collaborators, and that the nation could be built without their knowledge and expertise.

On the other hand, the progressive elements, including Pak Hun-young of the Korea Communist Party (later the Korea Labor Party), also argued persistently for the exclusion of pro-Japan groups. Both the conservatives and the progressives were in agreement on the principle (or justice) of excluding pro-Japan elements, but even so, a harsh political confrontation emerged between right and left wings over exactly how these pro-Japan elements should be treated.

The government promulgated the "Anti-Racial Activity Punishment Law" in 1948 to punish pro-Japan elements, but its stipulations were a poor match for both the spirit of justice and real-world conditions: 559 people were arrested, but only 221 were indicted, only 38 were tried, and 12 convicted. One was sentenced to death, and another was sentenced to life imprisonment (and released during the Korean War). Ten were sentenced to short terms in prison, 18 lost their voting rights, and 8 were acquitted.

Most police officers during that time of the Rhee government had served as police officers under the Government-General of

Korea. For this reason, the group most vehemently opposed to the Anti-Racial Activity Punishment Law was police officers. In fact, there was an incident where police officers opposing the law attacked the building that housed the investigation committee responsible for enforcing it.

Rhee Syng-man ignored this incident and did not pursue any criminal investigation. In fact, the chairman of this committee later said he had mistrusted the law from the outset. The committee functioned only from January to August 1949.

Many of the officers and soldiers of the military forces of Korea at that time were also military personnel under Japanese rule. The senior officers of the national security forces before the founding of South Korea (110 graduates from the Officers School for South Korea Security Guards guided by the U.S. Military Administration) were mainly men who had been student draftees, soldiers in Manchuria, and officers in the Japanese military.

Anti-Japan in public, pro-Japan in private

Rhee Syng-man was rigorous in his practice of anti-Japan ideology as the fundament of South Korean justice. He was thorough in integrating anti-Japan into the South Korean education system that denied Japanese rule. He was insistent in claiming Tsushima as Korean territory, and he unilaterally drew the so-called "Rhee Syng-man line" that imposed South Korea's practical control over Takeshima (Dok-do). However, he did not expel pro-Japan elements from the government. Instead, he used them in an important role to promote national reconstruction. Why he did so is clear. Korea's political, economic, and social systems had greatly modernized under Japanese rule, and Rhee Syng-man wanted to build on an advance in this modernization as he built a new nation.

But the conservatives never openly acknowledged the contribution that Japanese rule made to the modernization of Korea. Publicly, Rhee Syng-man totally rejected the legacy of Japanese rule, saying it represented "severely oppressive control and unchecked looting." He was vigorous in applying his anti-Japan doctrine based on the fabrication that the Korean people courageously fought for independence and against Japanese rule.

Then, on June 25, 1950, North Korea started the three-year Korean War, and the campaign to expel pro-Japan elements was suspended. South Korea as a new nation started out with fundamental contradictions. This is the most important point for understanding the anti-Japan policies that South Korea's conservative groups maintain even now.

In essence, it would have been better if South Korea's conservative groups had come to a more correct assessment that Japan had contributed to the modernization of the nation, and if they had sought the cooperation of the pro-Japan elements. This would have been the best route to the construction of a new nation. The reasons why they did not are spelled out below; if they had done this, the ideology of opposition to Japan as the basis of South Korean justice would have collapsed from the ground up, and its power might have shifted to the left-wing groups that opposed the United States, favored the Soviet Union and China, and advocated subjugation to North Korea.

From early on, it was this fundamental contradiction in the anti-Japan ideology of Rhee Syng-man and his associates, who opposed Japan publicly while embracing it privately, that held open the possibility for the left-wing groups to maintain any influence at all. The left-wing groups could say, truthfully, that conservative groups were publicly denouncing Japan while stopping short of punishing pro-Japan elements, allowing them to carry on their activities. The right's public face (principle) was anti-Japan, but its private face (true intention) was pro-Japan. That is why the left's argument was so convincing.

Rhee Syng-man and his conservative associates should have clarified their stance by reviewing problems that Korea faced before it came under Japanese rule, openly acknowledged Japan's contribution to Korea's modernization during the period of colonial rule, and honestly evaluated the favorable and harmful effects of Japanese rule on Korea. After completing a reviewing process like that, Rhee Syng-man and his associates could have debated squarely with the left. The fact that Rhee Syng-man and his associates did not do that opened the opportunity for the left to effectively criticize the right and led to the history of severe conflicts between conservative and progressive groups that continues even today.

Rhee Syng-man's anti-communism, and the April 3, 1948, incident when 30,000 people were murdered in Jeju-do

Rhee Syng-man publicly announced his anti-Japan stance at the same time as he pronounced his anti-communist policy. However, his anti-communist policy was much stronger than his anti-Japan stance. He earned his PhD at Princeton University, and he understood democracy very well. He thoroughly opposed communism in order to make Korea a democratic nation, to say nothing of other countries. South Korea's government needed to eliminate North Korean spying, guerrilla activities, incitement of public unrest, and related activities. This anti-communist policy was not just ideology; it had real-world implications, and Rhee Syng-man was unstinting in his pursuit of communists and their left-wing associates.

To control left-wing riots, Rhee Syng-man brought in the military to unhesitatingly and at times brutally suppress them, which resulted in the deaths of many who had nothing to do with the riots. In all, these incidents took hundreds of thousands of lives. These facts, I believe, are not well known outside Korea.

Toward the end of the Lee Dynasty in Korea, before the take-over by Japan, peasant riots, revolts, and uprisings were frequent throughout the nation. Obviously, these were a response to tyrannical government and harsh living conditions. Each time, the government mobilized the military and thoroughly suppressed these revolts. Many peasants who had nothing to do with the riots became victims of the suppression.

After Japan annexed Korea, there were no more peasant up-risings or revolts, with the sole exception of the independence movement of March 1, 1919. After Japan's rule ended, peasant riots and revolts resumed, often associated with the conflict be-tween North and South Korea. Rhee Syng-man resorted to the same kind of complete suppression that Korea had seen under the Lee Dynasty.

The first large-scale riot, in 1948, is often referred to as the Jeju 4.3 Incident. Left-wing groups, objecting to South Ko-rean elections, instigated a riot. Rhee Syng-man, who held the real power under the U.S. military administration, deployed the Korean military to suppress the insurrection. The incident was unusually large in scale. Some estimate that 30,000 of Jeju-do's 200,000 residents were killed through 1957.

During the period of Japanese rule, many people from Jeju-do belonged to Japan's Communist Party, and they carried out anti-Japanese activities in Japan. After World War II, they returned to Jeju-do and joined Korea's Labor Party (previously the Commu-nist Party). They solicited members and carried on guerrilla activ-ities, instigating a riot with 300 armed militants and 3,000 party members. At that time, many residents of the island did not un-derstand the essence of communism or democracy. They became Labor Party members because their friends were members. They became victims of the violent incidents. It was the adventurism of the left wing that was responsible.

The essential nature of these mass murders was the gruesome legacy of the Lee Dynasty's cruel tyranny. Every family member of those who participated in the riots was murdered. Families were wiped out, with no blood relatives surviving. Villagers who assisted the rioters, however slightly, could not escape the government's murderous suppression, and they perished.

The cruel system of secret reporting that forced villagers to betray their fellow villagers, leading to torturous interrogations, beheadings, and defilement of corpses, was a method of suppression practiced in the Lee Dynasty that was essentially revived in the Jeju 4.3 Incident. Nothing of this kind ever happened under Japanese rule.

The tradition of cruel suppression to maintain the government's power resurfaced in Korea after World War II. Rhee Syng-man, who advocated democracy, and Kim Il-song, who advocated communism, were alike in this regard. The South Korean government's policies aimed at the destruction of communist influences became terror politics and sparked mass anti-government movements in many regions of the country. The government's efforts to quash the left only pushed many people into the arms of the left.

At that time, many people thought of Japan and Western nations as imperialistic, war-mongering powers, and believed the Soviet Union and China to be peace-loving nations, contrary to the fact. Such delusions greatly influenced the thinking of communists and leftist groups advocating democracy. For them, to oppose war meant to oppose Japan and the United States, while to embrace peace meant to embrace the Soviet Union and China.

The same can be said of North Korea, even though it is difficult to understand this now. For a long time, even in Japan, many people thought of North Korea as a "workers' paradise." Some say that Japan might have had a communist government if Allied Supreme Commander Douglas MacArthur had not issued an order to stop a general strike just before it was to be implemented on February 1, 1947. The situation in Korea was much more serious.

Mass murder in the Guidance Association Incident and the "Gou-chang Incident"

In October 1948, right after Rhee Syng-man became president, he sent the military to suppress a rebellious military group that was angered by the suppression of the 4.3 Incident in Je-ju-do. The rebel group members were all killed, along with 8,000 unarmed civilians. This is referred to as the Yeousu-Sunchon Rebellion. Park Chung-hee, who later became president, was actually a member of the rebel group, and a military tribunal sentenced him to death. However, his sentence was later commuted thanks to his secret report on communists within the rebel group, and he returned to military service around the time the Korean War broke out.

The most horrible events were a series of mass murders that took place during the Korean War (June 1950–July 1953). On orders from Rhee Syng-man, South Korean military and police murdered many thousands of village residents, young and old, male and female, to destroy partisans they feared were communists or supporters of communists. The military and police forces carried out the mass murder of an estimated hundreds of thousands to 1.2 million people they regarded as dangerous elements, including many communists who had received supervision and re-education.

Here are some of the important details.

- June 25, 1950: The Korean War started when North Korea invaded South Korea.

- June 27, 1950: Rhee Syng-man fled Seoul after ordering the execution of people who were registered with the People's Guidance Association and associates of the South Korean Labor Party. The Guidance Association was an organization to re-educate former communists and their families. South Korean military and police mass-murdered people who were registered with the Guidance Association and political criminals in Daejun Prison (Guidance Association Incident). Similar murders were committed in prisons located in Busan, Masan, Jeju, Jinju, and other villages. In one village, the Korean military gathered local residents and murdered them with machine guns.

- July–September 1950: The Korean military murdered villagers in Gyeongsangbukdo Yeongcheon and in the vicinity of Nakdonggang.

- February 8, 1951: The Korean military gathered villagers and murdered them in 12 villages in two counties. From February 9 to 11, the Korean military murdered residents in Chirisan in Gyeongsang Namdo Gouchang, with most of the victims under the age of 15 (Gouchang Incident).

Rhee Syng-man told the public that North Korea was blamed for all these incidents. In January 1951, more than 90,000 South Korean soldiers starved or froze to death because senior officers

of the military reserves (a secondary military organization, re-
served for emergencies) embezzled military supplies and food.

As the military committed mass murders of civilians and the
corruption of the military leadership victimized many others,
young officers grew seriously concerned and felt a keen need to
reform the military regime. These young officers started to criticize their senior leaders, who only obeyed orders from Rhee
Syng-man. Many people sympathized with the young officers.
The Korean Army headquarters conferred with the U.S. military
about a possible coup that might overthrow Rhee Syng-man. At
the same time, the U.S. military was moving in the direction of
bringing the war to a cease-fire, while Rhee Syng-man was insistent on pressing forward. As the U.S. military was making plans
to remove Rhee Syng-man from power, senior leaders of the Korean military expressed support for the U.S. thinking.

In the meantime, North and South Korea negotiated a cease-
fire. On January 18, 1952, Rhee Syng-man introduced the "Rhee
Syng-man line," unilaterally declaring that Takeshima (Dok-do)
was a Korean territory.

This pattern of harsh, hard-line policies has hardly changed
in the intervening decades. The government of South Korea has
always taken an aggressive anti-Japan stance under two sets of circumstances: One is when failures of government policy cause public support for the government to decline precipitously. The other
is when the influence of North Korea and its advocates becomes
so great that the government feels its existence is threatened. At
such times, the South Korean government tries to deflect public
attention away from itself to an external adversary (Japan).

Rhee Syng-man's dictatorship and its collapse

As soon as the Republic of Korea was founded in 1948, the National Assembly elected Rhee Syng-man president, in accordance with the constitutional process. Over the next few years, however, criticism from political circles and the military establishment mounted, the political situation became less stable, and it became unclear if Rhee Syng-man would be reelected in 1952.

Rhee Syng-man was convinced his chances of re-election would improve if the president were elected directly by the people instead of the National Assembly. He was confident of this because he was the president who had stopped the North Korean invasion, who had declared the Rhee Syng-man Line, and who had made it clear he was willing to have a face-to-face confrontation with Japan. On top of that, the people of South Korea believed that North Korea's military had committed mass murder in South Korea.

From this point forward, Rhee Syng-man's regime became increasingly tyrannical and dictatorial.

- July 4, 1952: Rhee Syng-man declared martial law in Busan, where the government had relocated temporarily. He ordered the arrest of politicians from opposition parties and posted police officers all around the National Assembly Building. Under these conditions, with conservatives now making up the great majority of the participating members of the National Assembly, the body voted to revise the constitution to institute a direct election of the president by the people of South Korea.

- August 5, 1952: Rhee Syng-man won a landslide re-election as president. During the election, he mobilized police to obstruct supporters of the opposition party's vice-presidential candidate.
- July 27, 1953: North Korea and South Korea signed a ceasefire agreement.
- November 27, 1954: Rhee Syng-man and the ruling Liberal Party submitted to the Assembly a draft revision of the constitution, making the first president of the Republic alone immune to the provision barring presidents from serving for a third term. Adopting the revision required a two-thirds majority, or 135.33 votes, but the party won only 135. However, the Speaker of the Assembly, who supported Rhee Syng-man, argued that 135.33 could be rounded down to 135, and declared the revision to be adopted.
- May 15, 1956: Rhee Syng-man was elected for a third term as president, but Chang Myon of the opposition Democratic Party was elected vice president. On September 28, a retired military man's plan to assassinate Chang Myon was exposed before it was carried out.
- April 30, 1959: The newspaper *Kyunghyang Shinmun*, which supported Chang Myon, was forced to shut down. Rhee Syng-man's long-time political nemesis, Cho Bong-am, was executed as a North Korean spy.
- March 15, 1960: While campaigning for his fourth term as president, Rhee Syng-man organized campaign activities by public officials and ordered the police to monitor their activities. He engaged in illegal activities such as making fake

voting boxes, printing bogus ballots, and counting counterfeit votes. As a result, he won the presidential election handily, and his close ally, Lee Ki-boong, father of Rhee Syng-man's adopted son, was elected vice president.

As Rhee Syng-man and Lee Ki-boong, through their openly illegal campaign activities, won election, the Democratic Party's branch office in Masan, Gyoungsang Namdo, declared a boycott of the election. This sparked demonstrations denouncing the illegal and fraudulent election activities. The police shot at demonstrators, and 8 died, while more than 50 were injured. Demonstrations spread from Masan to other areas throughout the country.

On April 19, 1960, tens of thousands of people demonstrated in Seoul. In other major cities, students clashed with police, resulting in the deaths of 186 people. This is known as the 4.19 Revolution. Rhee Syng-man declared martial law and tried to mobilize the military. However, the U.S. military administration put pressure on the Korean military, and it did not respond to Rhee Syng-man's orders.

On April 20, U.S. ambassador to South Korea Walter McConaughy told the South Korean government that if Rhee Syng-man did not respond to the people's demands for his resignation, the United States would cancel President Dwight Eisenhower's visit and reconsider U.S. economic aid to South Korea. On April 23, Rhee Syng-man said he would step down as head of the administration and retain only his duties as head of the state. Demonstrators responded by demanding that Rhee Syng-man leave all his political positions.

Rhee Syng-man declared emergency martial law in major cities throughout South Korea, but the demonstrations did not let up, and the military declined to take serious measures to quell them. On April 25, about 30,000 demonstrators demanded Rhee Syng-man's resignation. On April 26, Rhee Syng-man's bronze statue in Pagoda Park was knocked down, and the residence of Vice President Lee Ki-boong was attacked. The National Assembly voted unanimously to demand the immediate resignation of President Rhee.

Rhee relented, and the dictatorship collapsed. Minister of Foreign Affairs Hu Jung became head of the cabinet and on April 27 temporarily positioned himself to exercise presidential power. On April 28, Rhee Syng-man's adopted son, Lee Gang-souk, shot and killed his biological father and other family members and then shot himself. Early on the morning of May 29, Rhee Syng-man and his wife boarded a plane that took them into exile in Hawaii.

The unfortunate reality in South Korea at that time was that if Rhee Syng-man had not wielded dictatorial power, pro-North elements would surely have wrested control.

It was impossible to hope that democracy would emerge without the support of a middle class, which Korea did not yet have. Only left-wing elements that viewed North Korea as a peace-loving country were in a position to press for reforms.

Most Japanese think of Rhee Syng-man as a staunch opponent of Japan because of his one-sided action in claiming Korean possession of Takeshima (Dok-do). In reality, however, he was an anti-communist who strove unrelentingly to eliminate communist influences by cooperating with pro-Japan elements when it suited him, while openly espousing his opposition to Japan.

For Rhee Syng-man and his associates, the confrontation with North Korean sympathizers in South Korea was nothing short of a civil war. While we can never approve of Rhee Syng-man's policies, which harmed so many innocent victims, we need to accept that nations around the world go to war with enemies both inside and outside their own boundaries. Noncombatants are often hurt and even killed in the process. War is a necessary evil for the elimination of enemies. This is the situation in which Rhee Syng-man found himself. The background that allowed Rhee Syng-man to unhesitatingly pursue such unprecedentedly brutal measures was the dictatorial legacy of the Lee Dynasty.

Group favoring subjugation to the North expands its influence, reformist military officers fear crisis

After Rhee Syng-man resigned, the National Assembly revised the constitution and adopted a parliamentary system. On May 19, 1960, National Assembly parliamentarians elected Yun Bo-seon president. Under the new parliamentary system, the president was only a figurehead and did not wield the power of the executive branch. Prime Minister Chang Myon of the Liberal Party held the real power.

In the invasion by North Korea, many soldiers and private citizens lost their lives. Pro–North Korean elements and loyalists who opposed the dictatorship of Rhee Syng-man were gaining wide support among the people. The left, which had been suppressed by the Rhee government, experienced a resurgence after that government collapsed.

The left-leaning Democratic Party won a landslide victory in the general election in July. This marked the beginning of South Korea's democratization, but it also brought South Korea closer to the North. After the Democratic Party's victory, conservative parties toned down their anti-communist, anti–North Korea policy stance, and a new political movement with the support of pro–North Korea and North Korea loyalists made a new beginning.

The Korea Teachers United Labor Union was formed in July. Other labor unions sprang up. In November, the United Association of Korea Labor Unions was formed. South Korea was one of the poorest nations in the world, and its gross domestic product (GDP) per capita was lower than North Korea's. Naturally, labor unions started under the protection of North Korea loyalists and communists who were calling for the overthrow of capitalist nations.

In August, North Korea's Kim Il-sung proposed the establishment of a "South-North Federation of Korea" as a transitional arrangement. In September, left-wing groups in South Korea responded to this proposal by forming the "People's Independent United Central Council."

As the slogans of the People's Independent Union rang out at meetings and demonstrations in many parts of Korea, the country fell into chronic political disorder and confusion.

When Rhee Syng-man was in power, he controlled the military well, but military leaders colluded with Liberal Party politicians and fell into the trap of corruption. It was commonly believed that the influence of North Korea supporters would only increase. Reflecting this sense of crisis, a group of military officers engaged energetically to reform the military establishment. The leader of the group was Park Chung-hee, who was esteemed for his integrity. Another top representative of the group was Kim Jong-pil.

The group appealed to Chang Myoun's newly appointed minister of defense, saying that the government should clean up the military "in the spirit of the 4.19 Revolution." But their appeal fell on deaf ears. Both within the military and among the general public, expectations of a coup d'etat became widespread. Private citizens took it as an open secret that the military was planning some kind of coup.

Officers in the military reformist group had a strong sense of indignation against the corrupt military leaders and also against the government that continued to fail to modernize the country in ways that might alleviate poverty. At the same time, these officers shared a sense of crisis that aggressive left-wing groups would seize power and promote the unification of Korea. They feared the nation was heading toward communism. These officers were convinced the nation was facing a life-or-death crisis, and that is what compelled them to stage a military coup.

Prime Minister Chang Myoun received numerous warnings of a military mutiny. But control of the South Korean military lay in the hands of the UN military administration commander. Prime Minister Chang Myoun continued to believe there was "nothing to worry about."

5.16 military coup and transition to military government

On May 13, 1961, the People's Independent United Central Council and student organizations held a meeting of the "Welcoming South-North Students Consultation and Conference of United Front for Progress." On May 20, the South-North Student Meeting was to take place in Panmunjom, bringing together students from North and South Korea. On that day, a large-scale demonstration from Seoul to Panmunjom was also planned.

It was four days before the South-North Student Meeting that the reformist military group carried out its coup. Depending on developments in Panmunjom, they feared that the U.S. military might take action, sparking a reaction by North Korea and escalating into another military confrontation.

On May 16, 1961, 3,600 soldiers rose up. The main groups were the Navy's First Brigade and the Air Force's First Airborne Combat Unit, supported by the 30th and the 33rd Reserve Divisions and the 6th Army Corps's Artillery Brigade. President Yun Bo-seon said, "The time has come." The great majority of the people silently acquiesced to the coup. The same can be said of the South Korean military.

The army chief of staff had been told in advance about the coup but took no action to prevent it. Instead, the military police guarding Seoul's Han-gang Bridge were denied heavy firepower (heavy machine guns, automatic cannons, large cannons, etc.). The chief of staff ordered them to keep lanes open on the bridge for cars to pass. Obviously, the military leadership tacitly approved of the coup. (Lee Younghun, [History of Korea], [Giparang])

The coup troops exchanged fire with about 50 military policemen for a short time near Han-gang Bridge, but the coup met no other resistance as it advanced into Seoul. Without difficulty, the coup troops took control of the National Assembly Building, central government offices, Army Headquarters, and the Broadcasting Bureau. When the coup leaders went to the Presidential Palace, the president said he would approve the coup. (Lee Younghun, op. cit.)

The coup group immediately organized the Military Revolutionary Committee, with the army chief of staff as president, and it broadcast the committee's declaration and its basic principles. The committee imposed martial law and on May 19 changed its name to the Supreme Conference for Nation Rehabilitation.

Carter B. Magruder, commander of the UN Force in Korea, and Marshall Green, acting ambassador of the U.S. Embassy in Korea, said they could not approve of the coup and announced support for the Chang Myoun government. Magruder demanded that the Korean military force come back under the command of the United Nations and ordered the Korean military to control the coup troops. However, the South Korean president did not accede to these demands.

On May 18, the Chang cabinet approved emergency martial law and then resigned. President Yun Bo-seon remained president.

On May 22, the United States agreed to the establishment of the Supreme Conference for National Rehabilitation organized by the coup troops, while continuing to say the coup was regrettable. The United States recognized that the objectives of the Supreme Conference were to support the UN, reform society, and return to constitutional government.

President Yun resigned in March 1962, and a military government was established with Park Chung-hee as president of the Supreme Conference for National Rehabilitation, which endured until December 1963.

Evaluation of the coup and the restoration regime

A year later, Park Chung-hee, as president of the Supreme Conference for National Rehabilitation, gave his reasons for carrying out the coup.

"The governments of the Republic of Korea over the years since its establishment have continued to be engaged in fights among political parties for selfish objectives, and have been in extreme corruption through the use of financial assistance from abroad. They not only ignored the people's suffering and poverty, but also expressed their call for friendly relations with North Korea and dragged the nation into a critical situation." (from *The Path that South Korean People Must Take*)

In Japan, the conventional wisdom has it that a military coup, a military government, and government based on martial law are bad. In developing countries, however, it is also true that, in nearly every case, military governments that carry out coups also implement revolutions or reforms. There are a number of reasons for this. One of the most important reasons is that elite groups— the traditional master class, landlords, the new capitalist class, government bureaucrats—vie with each other for power, fighting blindly for their own interests, while ignoring the needs of ordinary people. As a result, the vast majority of people fall into misery.

This creates conditions that encourage the spread of governments based on terror, rendering democratic elections impossible. This was the situation in South Korea under Rhee Syng-man. How else could South Korea's per capita GDP have been lower than North Korea's?

Park Chung-hee's aims in leading the military coup were to help people who were trapped in poverty while guarding them against the threats posed by North Korea, which was taking advantage of South Korea's disorder and confusion and making military advances. As Park Guen-hye has said, the coup was an unavoidable option and a bid to save the nation.

Park Chung-hee promised to end the military government in about two and a half years, and that is what he did, embarking on democratic government. In August 1963 he retired from the military and ran for president in the election scheduled on October 15. He won, decisively defeating former president Yun Bo-seon. He was reelected for a second term in May 1967 and for a third term in April 1971.

In his third electoral campaign, Park Chung-hee was seriously challenged by Kim Tae-jung of the opposition New Democratic Party and barely managed to win. Opposition parties outnumbered the ruling party in the National Assembly, and if the opposition parties could form a coalition, the ruling party was at risk of being defeated.

It was at this point that Park Chung-hee concluded that his vision of the nation's reform was incompatible with democracy, and he opted to form a dictatorship to achieve his reforms.

Park Chung-hee must have feared that if Kim Tae-jung and his leftist associates came to power, pro–North Korea elements and North Korea loyalists would become more influential, making another coup inevitable.

In October 1972, Park Chung-hee declared emergency martial law throughout South Korea (the "October Restoration"). In November, he held a national referendum for constitutional change, which led to the actual revision of the constitution, which changed the way presidential elections were held. Under the revised constitution, presidential elections were based on the People's Conference of United Constituents, comprising three pillars:

- Members of the People's Conference of United Constituents are chosen through national elections.
- Members of the People's Conference of United Constituents are prohibited from joining political parties.
- The People's Conference of United Constituents chooses one-third of the National Assembly members from candidates on a list recommended by the president.

On December 15, an election was held to choose representatives for the People's Conference of United Constituents, and the Conference chose Park Chung-hee as president of South Korea on December 27. Six years later, the election to choose representatives for the Second People's Conference of United Constituents was held on May 18, 1978, and Park Chung-hee was reelected as president on July 6.

The rules for these two elections allowed virtually no election campaigning, and government interference kept many opposition members from registering their candidacy.

The restoration regime that started in October 1972 was obviously a dictatorial system. But as Park Guen-hye has said, it was unavoidable, because it was the best option available to the president for saving the nation.

In its basic nature, the restoration regime was a "dictatorship for development." In other words, the regime needed to restrict popular participation in politics to secure the political stability needed for economic development.

Like military coups, this sort of regime can often be seen in developing countries. By having this type of regime for a time, South Korea was able to achieve rapid economic growth and escape from poverty.

In many developing countries, the military is the only force that can control all interest groups and exercise political power. The people often endorse arrangements like this, and it is not rare for military coups to be followed by dictatorships with popular support. In reality, it is not possible for any nation languishing in poverty to reform on its own, from the bottom up, through democratic coordination driven by the middle class.

Anti-Japan education took root during Park Chung-hee's presidency

During World War II, Park Chung-hee served in the Japanese military in Manchuria. He graduated from a Japanese military academy in 1942 and was known by a Japanese name. During his presidency, he did not reject people who were pro-Japan. In fact, he continued to employ, in important roles, holdovers from the Rhee Syng-man regime who held pro-Japan views.

His foreign policy on Japan steered clear of the Japan-Korea territorial issue, and he agreed with Japan that this issue should stay on the shelf. In June 1965, he concluded the Japan-Korea Basic Agreement, normalizing relations between South Korea and Japan. He also concluded the Japan-Korea Right of Claim and Economic Cooperation Agreement. Under this agreement, Japan agreed to provide grants, loans, and private-sector cooperation totaling $1.1 billion (about one-third of South Korea's 1965 GDP), and South Korea abandoned its rights of claim against Japan.

Regarding the Takeshima (Dok-do) problem, at a meeting in 1965, Park Chung-hee told U.S. Secretary of State Dean Rusk he would like to blow up the island to solve the problem. Regarding Japan's annexation of Korea, his understanding was that the Korean people themselves had chosen it. More on this later.

In his energetic pursuit of national restoration, agricultural reform, and rapid economic growth, as well as the specific details of his renovation policy, Park Chung-hee was openly modeling his policies on Japan's recent modernization.

For these reasons, many people in media and political circles in Japan saw Park Chung-hee as pro-Japan. Even so Park Chung-hee continued Rhee Syng-man's anti-Japan education policy and spread it even more widely throughout South Korea.

Park Chung-hee served as president for 16 years, from December 1963 through October 1979. The entire time, he remained unrelenting in promoting anti-Japan education. This is why people in South Korea are so tenacious in their anti-Japan sentiment.

Although anti-Japan education started during the reign of Rhee Syng-man, the people were poor in those years, and the level of education was very low, so anti-Japan sentiment was not widespread among the people. Only in 1954 did South Korea introduce free, compulsory education and a national, standardized primary education system. In 1960, when the Rhee Syng-man government collapsed, primary school attendance reached 95 percent, but the percentage of primary school graduates advancing to middle school was still very low.

During the presidency of Park Chung-hee, middle school enrollment increased rapidly. This was due mainly to the rapid economic growth that was achieved during that period. In 1984, under President Chun Doo-hwan, compulsory education was extended to middle schools. Starting that year, free compulsory middle-school education was introduced incrementally, until it was in practice throughout the nation by 2004.

In sum, Park Chung-hee instituted the anti-Japan slant in the South Korean education system, and anti-Japan propaganda was disseminated throughout the country through school education and mass media. That is how the current bias against Japan took root in South Korea. Until his death, Park Chung-hee himself remained anti-Japan in public but pro-Japan in private. He never relinquished the anti-Japan policy as his official doctrine.

Suppression of democracy movement, and North Korea's guerrila actions

The dictatorship came to an end during the presidency of Park Chung-hee's successor, Chun Doo-hwan. The major events of this transition are shown below:

- October 26, 1979: President Park Chung-hee was assassinated by KCIA Director Kim Jae-gyu. The following day, emergency martial law was declared throughout the nation, except Jeju-do. Prime Minister Choi Kyu-hah stepped in as presidential proxy. On December 12, Chun Doo-hwan, Roh Tae-woo, and other mid-level military officers assumed control over the military by arresting the army chief of staff and his associates (the military leadership), accusing them of involvement in the assassination (12.12 Military Reform Coup).
- May 18, 1980: The martial law command arrested Kim Tae-jung, Kim Jong-pil, Lee Hoo-lak, and 23 others, and put Kim Young-sam under house arrest. The command once again imposed martial law, including restriction of political activities, prior censorship of publications and broadcasting, and closure of universities. From May 18 to 27, citizens and students demonstrated in Gwangju. The city was under mil-

itary control, and about 200 people were killed (Gwangju Uprising).

- September 1, 1980: Chun Doo-hwan was officially inaugurated as the 11th president of South Korea.
- October 17, 1980: President Chun Doo-hwan abolished all political parties.
- January 1981: President Chun formed his own party, the Democratic Justice Party.
- February 25, 1981: Chun Doo-hwan assumed office as the 12th president of South Korea.
- In 1985, Mikhail Gorbachev became general secretary of the Communist Party of the Soviet Union and embarked on the policy of "perestroika" (openness). In South Korea, demands for democratization became even louder, and the Chun Doo-hwan government shifted emphatically toward democratization.
- June 26, 1987: More than 1 million citizens participated in a peaceful demonstration for a democratic constitution. On June 29, the government announced the June 29 Democratization Declaration, providing for the direct election of the president, the release of political prisoners, freedom of speech, greater autonomy for regional governments, and guarantees of academic independence. In October, a new constitution was adopted, and Roh Tae-woo was elected president.
- January 1988: Roh Tae-woo said the Gwangju Uprising represented "efforts for democratization."
- February 1988: Roh Tae-woo took office as president.

- September 1991: South Korea and North Korea joined the United Nations.
- August 1992: China and South Korea signed a treaty establishing diplomatic relations.
- December 1992: Kim Young-sam was elected president.

Kim Young-sam took office as president on February 25, 1993. Every civilian government since that time has maintained that previous dictatorship governments completely suppressed South Korea's struggle for democratization based on government pretenses of anti-communism and opposition to North Korea.

Under Park Chung-hee, for example, the government imposed martial law in Seoul and arrested 1,200 people when more than 10,000 students demonstrated against the Japan-Korea Basic Treaty (6.3 Incident). The government executed eight members of the People's Revolutionary Party for instigating "disturbances." Chun Doo-hwan and his associates suppressed the Gwangju Uprising, resulting in the deaths of about 200 people.

It has been said that the Gwangju Uprising and the People's Revolutionary Party Incident represented "suppression of democratic struggles." However, a former member of the People's Revolutionary Party has testified that "the People's Revolutionary Party indeed existed and its aim was to revolt against the nation." Regarding the Gwangju Uprising, an escapee from North Korea has testified that North Korean military forces instigated riots and interfered in the affairs of South Korea. It is impossible to separate "suppression of democratic struggles" from fighting back against North Korea's many terrorist and invasion activities.

On January 21, 1968, in the so-called "Blue House Raid,"

North Korean guerrillas infiltrated into Seoul in an attempt to assassinate Park Chung-hee. On August 15, 1974, a Korean national living in Japan named Moon Se-guan, acting under orders from North Korea, shot at Park Chung-hee, but killed Park's wife instead.

On October 9, 1983, North Korean terrorists attempted to kill President Chun Doo-hwan in Yangon, Myanmar, with a bomb. Seventeen South Koreans were killed, including cabinet members, and four Burmese government officials also died. The South Korean government's "suppression of pro-democratic struggles" occurred in a conflict with North Korea, which openly deployed soldiers and carried out terrorism in South Korea. These incidents occurred under the tense circumstances prevailing at the time. Later statements by civilian governments calling these actions unilateral suppression of freedom and democracy by a tyrannical government fail to take these circumstances into account.

Park Chung-hee's reconstruction of the nation started from self-criticism and reflection

South Korea's military presidents' understanding of history was clearly different from its civilian presidents' understanding. Park Chung-hee's understanding of Japan's annexation of Korea was that this was the choice of the Korean people. He often said this when he met with Japanese politicians.

"We chose (the annexation to Japan) by ourselves. It was not the case that Japan invaded (Korea); our ancestors chose (it). Had we chosen the Qing Dynasty, the dynasty would have been destroyed soon and a more chaotic situation would have prevailed throughout the Korean Peninsula. Had we chosen Russia, our country would have been destroyed soon after. Then, the Korean Peninsula would have been communized, with North and South Korea under the complete control of the communists. The fact that we chose Japan cannot be described as the best option, but I believe that it was our second best as we had no other option." (Shintaro Ishihara, "Japan! Believe in Yourself, and Open Your Own Destiny," *Monthly Seiron*, January 2003)

Park Chung-hee recanted Rhee Syng-man's ambiguous notion regarding "Independence Day," which he referred to as "Half-Liberation" because of U.S. military protection, and he said:

"August 15, 1945!! This is our national liberation anniversary day. However, we did not win national liberation on our own efforts. Rather, the Allies gave it to us as a gift at the end of the war, and it marked the start of 16 years of post-independence confusion." (Park Chung-hee, *The Path the Han Race Should Tread*)

For Park Chung-hee, the important point was not how Korea gained independence, but rather how the nation was rebuilt thereafter. Park Chung-hee took a critical view of the events that took place in the ensuing 16 years.

"We wasted years, intoxicated by the joy of gaining independence, unable to establish systems and self-reliance, while some 40 developing nations achieved their own independence and entry to the United Nations before we did." (*Collection of Statements by Park Chung-hee*, President of the National Reconstruction Supreme Conference and Acting President, Secretariat of the Presidential Office, 1965)

Park Chung-hee argued that the most important cause of Korea's annexation by Japan and of South Korea's collapse following its independence was the selfish intra-party factionalism that emerged from the 500-year history of the Joseon Dynasty. To overcome this, the Korean people must reform their character (*The Path that South Korean People Must Take*). He analyzed the "selfish intra-party factionalism" from three angles and pointed out problems the Korean people must overcome.

(1) Lack of racial pride. Korean people love themselves and have an extraordinary degree of loyalty and passion toward their "group" (party, faction), but they lack passion for their race.

(2) Sense of special privilege. Collective benefits, prosperity, and a sense of racial (national) unity have been hampered by an "elite" mentality where people are obsessed with having more money than others and being better in terms of academic background, lineage, or party clique.

(3) Party factionalism. In the past, parties' focus on their own interests and having their own policies implemented has distorted the path of national policy.

Park Chung-hee's aim was to construct a new nation through self-criticism and reflection on the shortcomings of the Korean people.

Anti-Japan education under the military governments

Chun Doo-hwan and Roh Tae-woo shared Park Chung-hee's ideas on self-criticism and reflection. On August 15, 1981, Chun Doo-hwan's Independence Day remarks included the following:

"The Allies' victory and Japan's defeat, which were both beyond the control of the Korean people, were another definitive factor contributing to the August 15 Independence for Korea. If there had been no such conditions that were beyond the control of the Korean people, we had had no other options but to pursue independence with our own efforts. If that had been the case, we would have needed to prepare ourselves to pay the price of more time and more sacrifices."

"Regarding our national shame that we lost our nation, we should not blame Japanese imperialism. Instead we should reflect on the circumstances prevailing at that time and on the weakness and strength in securing our domestic unity. We need to have the attitude to criticize ourselves." (*Collection of Remarks by Chun Doo-hwan*, Secretariat of the Presidential Office, 1983)

On May 25, 1990, Roh Tae-woo, on his first visit to Japan as president of Korea, delivered a speech in which he said:

"We should reflect on ourselves for the fact that we could not defend our nation in the past. We do not blame others or envy others" (press report).

Park Chung-hee, Chun Doo-hwan, and Roh Tae-woo all wanted to build a new nation based on "self-criticism and reflection." However, for domestic reasons, they continued the system of anti-Japan education started by Rhee Syng-man. And that is not all. Park Chung-hee never told the South Korean people that he was able to achieve rapid economic growth by using massive amounts of financial aid arranged through the normalization of relations with Japan.

One of my Japanese acquaintances, Mr. A., told me a story. President Park invited Mr. A. to come to South Korea. President Park wanted to give him an award for his great contribution to the construction of Pohang Steel Co. and Korea's economic development. Mr. A. went to the Blue House (presidential palace), wondering what the award ceremony would be like. The president quietly led Mr. A to his office. No one else was there. Just the two of them. The president handed Mr. A. a certificate. I believe this is a typical example of "anti-Japan in public and pro-Japan in private."

Here is another example. On August 15, 1987, Chun Doo-hwan opened the Independence Hall of Korea, a museum also known as the "Anti-Japan Museum," in the city of Chung-cheongnam-do. In the museum, there is a life-size wax exhibition that depicts "Japanese torture of Koreans" that did not actually exist. The cruelty shown by the exhibition makes you cover your eyes. Students from schools all over Korea come to see the exhibition, which reinforces the lessons of their anti-Japan education.

The most important point of this anti-Japan education pushed by Park Chung-hee, Chun Doo-hwan, and Roh Tae-woo is to make the Korean people believe how cruel Japanese imperialism was, and how well the Korean people persevered despite such humiliation. This is why the Independence Hall of Korea was built.

The purpose of anti-Japan education might have been for the Korean people to reflect on their own history, how they overcame their humiliations and became independent. Instead, anti-Japan education in South Korea led to the kind of anti-Japan sentiment filled with the fundamentally physiological hatred as I personally experienced.

Obviously, this anti-Japan education has been a fundamental mistake. I must conclude that building a new nation based on self-criticism and reflection was the wrong direction to take.

Chapter III

New Developments in Anti-Japan Ideology

Kim Young-Sam's "re-discipline Japan"

South Korea's civilian government was meant to be a reformist government with a new take on the military governments' legacy of self-criticism and reflection. However, when Kim Young-sam, the first civilian president (February 1993–February 1998), took office, he, too, failed to broach the truth that Korea's independence was the result of Japan's defeat and the Allies' victory in World War II, and that the Korean people had not won independence through their own efforts. He said only that independence had finally been completed and that the next challenge was to unite the nation.

As soon as he assumed the presidency, Kim Young-sam demolished the building that housed the former Japanese Government-General of Korea as a "vestige of Japanese imperialism." He said South Korea would no longer blame Japan for its colonial rule over Korea and that the leaders of the two countries should be silent about what Japan did in the Korean Peninsula (speech during the ceremony commemorating the 3.1 Independence Movements Anniversary).

Around the same time, Japanese Prime Minister Tomiichi Murayama said, "Japan inflicted great damage and suffering on the people in the Asian countries through its colonial controls and invasions," and he expressed a "keen sense of reflection on themselves" and "sincere apology." These statements, made on August 15, 1995, during a ceremony commemorating the 50th anniversary of the end of World War II, were the essence of what is known as the "Murayama Statement [of apology]."

Shortly after that, however, Kim Young-sam broke the unspoken agreement to keep the Takeshima (Dok-do) problem under wraps. He ordered the construction of a pier there and then stationed a permanent marine force on the island and began to fortify it with antiaircraft weapons.

In response to this South Korean action, Japanese Foreign Minister Yukihiko Ikeda said Takeshima is a Japanese territory, based on history and international law. He asked the South Korean government to stop construction of the pier. Kim Young-sam responded negatively to Ikeda's remarks. A large number of demonstrators gathered in front of the Japanese embassy in Seoul, burning a Japanese flag and an effigy of Ikeda. A storm of condemnation spread throughout South Korea.

Another large anti-Japan demonstration was held on October 5, 1996, when Prime Minister Murayama said in Parliament that the 1910 Japan-Korea Annexation Treaty had been legally valid.

Like Park Chung-hee, Kim Young-sam was also pro-Japan in private, but his public position was that he would "re-discipline Japan" with respect to the Takeshima (Dok-do) issue. At a meeting with Chinese leader Jiang Zemin, Kim Young-sam took an aggressively anti-Japan stance, saying he would "correct the bad habits of the Japanese."

Kim Tae-jung makes changes in Japan policy

President Kim Tae-jung (February 1998–February 2003) was the first South Korean president to say publicly that the Korean people had won their independence through their own efforts.

"We have a great history of struggle, unparalleled in the world, for our great independence. Throughout the entire period of Japanese imperialist rule, our ancestors persisted, without a day of rest, in their armed struggle. After the 3.1 Independence Movement, we defended the laws and rules of our transitional government. This is nothing but our proud history, which our race alone possesses" (press report on President Kim Tae-jung's speech during the ceremony commemorating the Independence Anniversary on August 15, 2001).

Around that time, the tone of textbooks containing anti-Japan education changed, now stating that the Korean people won their independence through their own struggle. This interpretation of history remains the norm today.

Why did Kim Tae-jung take this position?

The reason is that he wanted to paint a picture that the Korean people's struggle for democracy remained the same under Japanese colonial control and under the military regime of his presidential predecessors. His view was that the Korean people's struggle was the key to both ending domination by another race and ending dictatorship. The core value in his view of history was democracy. From that view emerged the equation "opposition to Japan equals democracy."

Even so, after taking office, Kim Tae-jung showed a certain understanding of Japan. He publicly announced that his government would refer to the Japanese emperor as emperor, rather than his predecessors' habit of calling him the Japanese "king." At an official dinner at the Imperial Palace, President Kim used no inflammatory words such as "colonial control." When Princess Aiko was born in 2001, he sent a congratulatory telegram with the message, "I join the Korean people in extending our sincere congratulations at the birth of an imperial grandchild that the Japanese Imperial Family and the people all longed for." He also publicly expressed, both in Korea and abroad, his support for Japan's efforts to become a permanent member of the UN Security Council.

When Kim Tae-jung visited Japan in October 1998, he and Prime Minister Keizo Obuchi released a joint statement. Prime Minister Obuchi expressed Japan's apology for the harm it had inflicted in the past, while Kim expressed great appreciation for Japan's international cooperation and economic aid since the 1965 normalization agreement. Kim Tae-jung was the first South Korean president to publicly praise Japan. He promised that the South Korean government would never again bring up matters of "past history," and he repeatedly said, "With my visit to Japan, the past has been cleared."

In 2001, however, the Japanese government approved a history textbook that South Korea said presented a distorted view of history. South Korea responded by criticizing Japan repeatedly and severely restricting private-sector cultural exchanges.

Kim Tae-jung was privately pro-Japan and publicly said the past was past, but in reality he, too, was enmeshed in the past.

Korea's currency crisis of November 1997 brought the nation to the brink of collapse. When Kim Tae-jung became president in 1998, there was a big shift in the tenor of anti-Japan ideology in South Korea. There were no more large demonstrations, even when the textbook issue arose. Some people in South Korea even objected to the restrictions on cultural exchanges. The main source of anti-Japan sentiment shifted to professional anti-Japan groups that engaged in extreme activities, threats, and aggressive statements. These no longer involved the president or the broad public, but lesser politicians and intellectuals, newspapers and TV, and extremist blogs on the Internet.

Roh Moo-hyun's affinity for North Korea, intensification of domestic opposition

Like his predecessors, at the beginning of his presidency Roh Moo-hyun (February 2003–February 2008) took a forward-looking posture on the Japan-Korea relationship. On his first trip to Japan he said, "We cannot be bound forever by the fetters of the past." He practiced "shuttle diplomacy" with Japan, paying frequent visits to Prime Minister Junichiro Koizumi.

Roh Moo-hyun's most important goal was to unify South and North Korea. He planned to continue and expand Kim Tae-jung's "sunshine policy." The first step would be to create a federation of the two Koreas. To find common ground, he stressed that South Korea's domestic reforms emphasize the importance of workers rather than corporations, income distribution rather than income growth, and the realization of democracy through the abolition of the National Security Law. He wanted to reproach the older generation and thought the real conclusion to be drawn about postwar Korea was that "left-wing anti-government activists should be seen as national loyalists who contributed to democracy." Roh Moo-hyun believed that Koreans who collaborated with the Japanese authorities during the colonial period should be reviled and socially shunned.

Roh Moo-hyun encouraged social-democratic policies and rapprochement with North Korea. North Korea loyalists and left-wing activists flourished. Public opinion was split, and hot debate raged throughout the country. On September 9, 2004, some 1,500 people, led by many current and former senior political leaders, gathered to express their impatience and criticism of President Roh and his government. They spoke out in favor of freedom and democracy.

In a "Declaration on the Current State of Affairs," the leaders said Korea was "currently facing great challenges with respect to its identity and national principles." They appealed to the president, the government, and the ruling party to immediately stop promoting an energy-sapping agenda that divided the nation and instead to focus on issues that need prompt solutions such as national security and the economy.

The statement went on to say that, unlike previous governments, President Roh's government pushed its agenda one-sidedly, without discussion with the people. "Korea faces great challenges with respect to its identity and national principle," it said.

The media, as typified by the newspaper *Chosun Ilbo*, said this statement was a useful tool of policy participation for the current and former senior leaders and intellectuals of Korea who had been critical of the government during the Reform Period of the 1970s and the military governments of the 1980s.

"The Declaration of the Current State of Affairs is a tool to reflect the inner voices of the people who lived during the 1970s and 1980s. During that period, the people felt superficially good as if they accomplished uniting the people of Korea and obtained harmony in the country, but in reality they experienced an inner turmoil of disintegration and confrontation. Here again we hear similar voices from the Declaration. What does that mean? It must be that Korean society is again falling into a period of disintegration." (*Chosun Ilbo*, September 9, 2004)

The current disintegration in South Korea reflects two antithetical positions that have emerged with respect to the nation's government and the way forward. On the one hand, there is left-wing nationalism favoring North Korea, the position taken by President Roh Moo-hyun and his Uri Party, and on the other hand the traditional, conservative, anti–North Korea stance of the opposition Grand National Party.

The senior leaders were anxious about President Roh's moves toward rapprochement with North Korea. President Roh seemed interested only in deepening friendly relations with the North, while ignoring Pyongyang's deplorable record on human rights, they said. His moves to abolish the National Security Law could be construed as toleration of North Korean spies and communist guerrillas.

Shift toward extreme anti-Japan posture

President Roh Moo-hyun shifted further in the anti-Japan direction in 2005, when details of the 1965 Japan-Korea Agreement came to light. Rights of claim and the Takeshima (Dok-do) problem emerged anew, as Japan's Shimane Prefecture asserted its own claim to the remote island. This turned public opinion in South Korea against the Japanese government's handling of these issues.

On February 23, 2005, former Japanese ambassador to Korea Toshiyuki Takano told journalists in Seoul that Takeshima is a Japanese territory, based on both law and historical evidence. The South Korean government protested strongly, saying Japan had ignited the fire on the issue.

President Roh, in an Independence Day speech on March 1, said, "If Japan realizes the truth in the past history, apologizes for it, and reflects on it, then Japan should compensate for it, and we would reconcile with each other." He added, "This is the standard way for the whole world to follow in order to clear off the past history." He said, "There is no other way for the Korean government to take responsibility for dealing with the issue of the individual's rights of claim, but at the same time Japan must understand the universal principle of the human society and the issue related to the trust among the neighboring countries and show positive attitude in this respect."

This was the first time any South Korean president publicly mentioned Japanese compensation since the conclusion of the Japan-Korea Normalization Treaty, and it meant a strongly anti-Japan shift in Roh Moo-hyun's policy stance. When Prime Minister Koizumi then visited Yasukuni Shrine, the shuttle diplomacy between Japan and Korea was put on hold, not to be resumed as long as Roh Moo-hyun remained in office.

In Korea, a series of raucous demonstrations protested Shimane Prefecture's decision to make March 16 "Takeshima Day." On March 17, Roh Moo-hyun gave a speech vilifying Japan as if it were South Korea's enemy. He stated four basic principles for South Korea's relations with Japan.

(1) Construction of a Korea-Japan relationship based on universal values and common sense shared by all human beings.

(2) Firm response to the Takeshima (Dok-do) problem and interpretation of history.

(3) Positive efforts in international forums to clarify South Korea's principles and concepts of justice.

(4) Maintenance of current programs in politics, foreign affairs, economy, society, cultural, and human exchanges.

He characterized Japanese history textbooks as approving Japan's past state power and invasion of Korea. He said Japan's assertions of sovereignty over Takeshima (Dok-do) were more than a territorial issue, they were an attempt to deny the history of Korea's liberation from Japanese colonization and to justify the past annexation. President Roh also broached the issue of compensation for "victims of Japan's colonial control," saying, "Regarding individual victims who suffered in connection with business outside the coverage specified by the Japan-Korea Normalization Agreement, the Japanese government is encouraged to settle the issue, taking into account respect for human rights."

Roh Moo-hyun and Secretary of Unification Chung Dong-young said they were finished with the traditional policy of "quiet diplomacy."

On March 18, Seoul asked Japan to "make earnest efforts in dealing with the distortions of history in the textbook published by the Japanese right-wing publishing company, Fusosha." According to the *Chosun Ilbo* (March 18, 2005), "Japan made no promise to rectify the situation." The City Council of Gyoung-sang Nam-do Ma-san protested Shimane Prefecture's declaration of "Takeshima Day" and announced its own counterclaim to the island of Tsushima in Japan's Nagasaki Prefecture. It announced "Tsushima Day" and said it would try to recover territory. The South Korean government and the Uri Party said they would consider drafting a law to demand that Japan compensate Korean comfort women.

On March 22, at the Military Academy graduation ceremony, Roh Moo-hyun suggested Seoul might "leave the Korea-U.S.-Japan alliance," which would "change the geopolitical situation in Northeast Asia."

At a town meeting on March 23, Roh said, "We can no longer ignore the Japanese government's justifying the history of Japan's invasion and control in the past as well as its intention to carry out its hegemony." He mentioned the Japanese prime minister's visit to Yasukuni Shrine, the local ordinance about Takeshima Day, and textbooks that distort history, and said these matters "completely nullified Japan's self-reflection and apology of previous years…. These actions were not limited to a regional government and a small group of nationalists. They were supported by the central government. We must reconsider our position on Japanese activity." The president's remarks that day included such saber-rattling phrases as "possibility of diplomatic war," "war that cannot be finished in a day or two," "we can no longer be silent," and "Korea will win." (*Dong-a Ilbo*, March 23, 2005)

No South Korean president before him had ever spoken about Japan in such strident terms. Roh Moo-hyun said he himself would fight on the front lines of diplomatic war against Japan. The newspaper *Dong-a Ilbo* said the president had his back to the wall.

Japan as "enemy of humanity"

The Korean government came precariously close to severing diplomatic relations with Japan. Then, the Korean press suddenly started to push back, publishing articles criticizing the harshness of the government's new anti-Japan stance.

Dong-a Ilbo published an editorial with the headline, "Doubts about Diplomatic Policy, President Himself Takes Front-Line Position":

"It cannot be wise of the president to make direct statements

with definitive expressions about every one of these subtle diplomatic issues.... President Kim Young-sam's remarks that he
would punish Japan had consequences for Korea-Japan relations.
... If the president, who is the final goalkeeper for national security, leaves his position and runs to the middle of the field, this
could cause a national crisis, increasing the chances of shaming
the country." (*Dong-a Ilbo*, March 23, 2005)

Another newspaper, *Chosun Ilbo*, published an article with the
headline, "President Roh Is Too Impatient; Critical Voices on
His Strong Anti-Japan Remarks." *Chosun Ilbo* quoted a former
president of the National Information Bureau as saying, "We can
understand there are situations in which the President cannot
simply sit silent, but this is no time for him to put himself on the
front line." (*Chosun Ilbo*, March 24, 2005)

These positions of the major newspapers echoed those of the
conservative political parties.

On April 5, the South Korean government expressed deep
concern that the Japanese government had approved middle-
school textbooks describing Takeshima (Dok-do) as Japanese
territory, and said it was firmly committed to dealing with the
issue. It also said that textbooks published by Fusosha and others rationalized and glorified past crimes. But it stopped short of
demanding that Japan revise the textbooks. The current government of Park Guen-hye has openly demanded that corrections be
made.

On April 7, South Korea's ambassador to the UN, Kim Sam-
hoon, told the General Assembly that Korea would oppose an
increase in the number of permanent members of the Security

Council. He was careful not to make direct reference to Japan, but it was obvious that Japan's ambitions were the object of Korea's ire.

On April 8, Kim Tae-jung told the leaders of the Uri Party, "If [the Takeshima issue] becomes excessively complicated, this would play into the hands of Japan, which would try to steer the controversy, and Korea would become entangled." He warned that President Roh Moo-hyun's aggressive unilateral approach could benefit Japan.

After receiving these warnings from the press and a former president, the government certainly returned to a search for "quiet diplomacy." President Roh himself, however, remained bellicose. On April 8, he told the *Frankfurter Allgemeine Zeitung*:

"Japan should be responsible for the steadily intensified dispute between Korea and Japan."

"Japan's attitude is not appropriate in light of the universal values that human society must pursue."

"It is a profound unhappiness for the entire world to live with people who think the past invasion and harm to be a source of pride." (Roh Moo-hyun interview with *Frankfurter Allgemeine Zeitung*, as quoted in *Chosun Ilbo*, April 8, 2005)

Chosun Ilbo opined that President Roh's remarks on the subject of Japan were his most severe yet. These were practically an ultimatum, painting Japan as an enemy. Roh likened Imperial Japan to Nazi Germany, saying both were "criminals against humanity." He then said that while Germany had come to terms with its history, Japan had not.

Roh Moo-hyun visited Germany in April 2005, where he

repeated his message about the need to base Korea-Japan relations on universal values and common sense and to clarify Korea's principles and concepts of justice. He again praised Germany for coming to terms with its history, and contrasted Germany with Japan. "Japan ... is contrary to the universal values shared by human beings."

He said visits to Yasukuni Shrine by Japanese government leaders were great insults to China as well as Korea, adding that Korea was ready to align itself with China to fight Japan's territorial claims and distortion of history. Prime Minister Koizumi reportedly sent a "letter of reconciliation" to Roh on April 8, the day Roh made these remarks. However, Roh still wanted to shame Japan in the international community.

Coming to terms with Korea's history of dictatorship

Since the establishment of civilian government in South Korea, "coming to terms with history" has been seen as the highest objective for the development of democracy in South Korea. "Coming to terms with history" means overcoming the heritage that has hindered the development of democracy. All civilian presidents from Roh Tae-woo to Kim Tae-jung were in accord on this. For Roh Moo-hyun, however, the subject came to include colonial control by Imperial Japan as well.

Concretely, this means confronting the violence, murders, character assassination, and other human rights violations committed in the name of the state under presidents Rhee Syng-man, Park Chung-hee, and Chun Doo-hwan. To come to terms with this history, the Roh Moo-hyun government pursued "investigation of the truth, punishment of responsible persons by the rule of law, economic assistance to victims, restoration of honor, abolishment of oppressive institutions, and reform of the laws and regimes that allowed the military governments' use of undemocratic practices in connection with those incidents."

Special laws were enacted regarding:

- The Jeju 4.3 Incident, where a large number of civilians were murdered by military forces in 1948, when the military suppressed riots by South Korea's Labor Party and left-wing groups protesting the election in Jejudo.

- The Geochang massacre, where the South Korean military murdered a large number of civilians during the Korean War under the pretext of "partisan extermination."

- The 5.18 Democracy Movements Incident and the Guangju Uprising, where a large number of citizens and students were killed in Guangju during the military's suppression of large-scale pro-democracy demonstrations in 1980.

- The Samcheong Educational Group Incident in 1980, where the government arrested and forced young people into the military and then abused them under the pretext of "social correction."

- The Nogeunri Incident in 1950, where the U.S. military mistakenly killed many civilians during the Korean War.

- The Suspicious Death Incidents, a group of incidents where many people were allegedly tortured to death in connection with pro-democracy movements.

- Special Duty, addressing needs for compensation and support for people who were tasked with special operations against North Korea.

- Police Special Duty to prevent the repatriation of Korean residents in Japan. In 1959, some people were tasked to perform special duty to destroy Japan Red Cross Center ships and trains used to repatriate Korean residents in Japan to North Korea.

Roh Moo-hyun's government promulgated the Framework Act on Clearing up Past Incidents for Truth and Reconciliation (May 31, 2005). This law aimed at pursuing truth regarding "national institutions' murder of civilians, suppression of human rights, and restoration of the honor of the victims." The government reviewed 11,160 cases, completing 9,987 cases by June 30, 2010, when the investigation ended.

Coming to terms with history without criticizing North Korea

With this one special law, the government carefully exposed, one by one, thousands of cases of human right violations committed by South Korea's dictatorial regimes and worked to compensate and restore the honor of people who were unjustly accused of crimes. The government used the power of the nation to come to terms with these liabilities of the country's history. This allowed the government in power to sit in judgment on preceding governments, according to the rule of law.

During the period of South Korea's dictatorship regimes, there were many incidents worthy of condemnation from a democratic standpoint. The reason for South Korean governments' turning dictatorial, however, is that South Korea had to confront North Korea, which wanted to unify through the use of military might. Since its establishment, North Korea has continued to send many spies to South Korea, inciting unrest in the country, carrying out guerrilla activities, committing terrorist acts, and planning military invasion. Had South Korea not forcibly removed pro–North Korea elements from within its own borders, it surely would have fallen under their control. Even if they did not approve of the dictatorships, many people in South Korea supported the idea of removing pro–North Korean elements.

Still, as South Korea came to terms with the historical liabilities of the dictatorial regimes, there was no consideration of North Korean influences. With a simple model of good vs. evil, where democracy equals good and dictatorship equals evil, the civilian government totally negated the dictatorial governments that had preceded it.

While most people sheepishly accepted as correct the idea of clearing off past misdeeds without criticizing North Korea, South Korea rapidly came under the sway of pro–North Korean elements and became willing to subjugate itself to North Korea.

The civilian government should have recognized that a democratic approach could not protect South Korea from sliding under the influence of North Korea. Also, the government should have acknowledged that the dictatorial regimes, through the use of force, had succeeded in protecting South Korea. "Coming to terms with history" needs to include facts like that, however uncomfortable. Instead, the civilian government only pointed accusatory fingers at the harm the dictatorships had caused, without understanding the factors that had made them necessary, the civilian government's own responsibility to accept the dictatorial past, and the benefits it had generated.

The same can be said about coming to terms with the history of Imperial Japan's colonial rule of Korea. If one substitutes the expression "Imperial Japan's colonial rule" for "dictatorship regime," the same conclusion emerges.

Reinventing history through "North–Koreanization"

In Japan, there are many perspectives on historical events, and this is accepted as normal. In South Korea, however, there is a tendency to set a national view and seek to establish it as the one true and correct view. A typical example would be the effort to completely negate Japan's rule over Korea during the period of annexation and colonization. Similarly, the nation aimed to establish a definitively correct view regarding South Korea's own period of dictatorship, centering on accounts of various salient incidents.

Here is a significantly problematic issue. The majority of incidents investigated were related to human rights violations that stemmed from the anti-communist and anti–North Korea policies pursued by the governments in power during the period concerned. The "coming to terms with liabilities from the past" was pushed mainly by the political agendas of Kim Tae-jung and Roh Moo-hyun, and naturally reflected the leanings of pro–North Korean elements.

This bias can be seen clearly in the implementation of the "Special Law to Find the Truth on Suspicious Deaths" (January 15, 2000). Roh Moo-hyun established a commission on the basis of this law (under the direct control of the president), which investigated a case involving the deaths of three long-term prisoners who had been sent by North Korea as spies to South Korea, as well as anti-government and communist guerrillas who had not yet been "converted." The commission determined that their deaths were suspicious and that they "had contributed to democracy in Korea," and it decided to restore their good name and bestow awards upon them.

These prisoners were not put in jail based on unjust accusations. They were accused of engaging in spying and guerrilla activities in South Korea. They had not been "converted." The conclusion that they contributed to democracy in South Korea is nothing more than an argument constructed by North Korea.

It is clear why this conclusion was reached. To begin with, Roh Moo-hyun appointed as a personal secretary to the president a person who had been an anti-government communist guerrilla. Moreover, the commission included a member who had served time in prison for being a North Korean spy.

Furthermore, the Uri Party, which was the ruling party at that time, widened its interpretation of the law to include the investigation of "incidents of death and disappearance caused by the inappropriate use of public power" and reopened the investigation of the KAL 858 explosion (November 1987, during the presidency of Chun Doo-hwan). This re-investigation concluded it was not North Korea that was behind the planting of the bomb that blew up the airplane; instead it was the South Korean government in power at that time. This conclusion was nothing but the argument advanced by North Korea.

It has been asserted that the aim of "coming to terms with the past" is the development of democracy in South Korea. However, the governments of Kim Tae-jung and Roh Moo-hyun condemned only human rights violations committed by South Korea, and never criticized or protested the many violations of human rights committed by North Korea. Like the "Sunshine Policy," the "coming to terms" policy was promoted by political groups that never questioned North Korea's nuclear development or human rights violations. This is a far cry from the goal of developing democracy in South Korea.

What happened instead was the fabrication of history along lines favoring North Korea. Kim Tae-jung and Roh Moo-hyun promoted a masochistic view of history that negated postwar South Korean history and accepted North Korean views.

Roh Moo-hyun comes to terms with history by negating pro-Japan elements

President Roh Moo-hyun pressed for a "coming to terms with

history" that included Imperial Japan's colonial rule. As mentioned earlier, the motive behind this policy was based on the idea that South Korea should not be satisfied with an anti-Japan ideology that was incomplete or just for public consumption. Roh Moo-hyun believed the dictatorial presidents had been too soft on pro-Japan elements.

In North Korea, the prevailing view was that Koreans who had collaborated with the Japanese during the period of colonial rule were evil criminals and traitors. South Korea also embraced anti-Japan ideology, but it regarded pro-Japan activities during the colonial period as something that resulted inevitably from the circumstances prevailing at that time. However, after Roh Moo-hyun came to power, he believed this traditional attitude stood in the way of "coming to terms with the past." He argued that South Korea, like North Korea, should punish those who "were engaged in pro-Japan activities during the period of Imperial Japan's control."

In South Korea, it is a national principle that pro-Japan equals unjust equals traitorous. Both ordinary people and intellectuals in South Korea seldom if ever question what is wrong with being "pro-Japan." Obviously, the correct argument has been that South Korea was wrong in the past for not punishing those who committed crimes. Reflecting this, in 2004 South Korea passed the Special Act on the Inspection of Collaborations under the Jopanese Occupation. This was later revised (January 27, 2005) to remove the expression "Pro-Japan." This change greatly widened the scope of investigation. Based on this law, the government of Roh Moo-hyun established the Commission on Investigation of

Truth regarding Pro-Japan and Anti-National Activities, under the direct control of the president, and promoted the "selection and investigation" of people suspected of being pro-Japan during the colonial period. This commission compiled reports and historical materials.

There were 25 categories of activities considered pro-Japanese and anti-national, including cooperation with the Japanese army as senior officials; promoting or advising the adoption of Japanese names; praising Japanese control and playing leadership roles in the campaign to unite Japan and Korea and make Koreans subjects of the Japanese emperor; producing military goods and providing materials to the Japanese Army; and acting on a Japanese local government advisory committee or legislative body. Later the commission published a list of persons (including the deceased) who were found to be anti-nation activists, and the commission punished these people as traitors.

Roh Moo-hyun promulgated another law—the Special Act for Returning the Property of Anti-National and Pro-Japanese Collaborators to the State (December 8, 2005)—allowing the government to forcefully claim assets owned by people found to have been pro-Japan and anti-Nation activists or their heirs. The government confiscated such assets from the end of 2005 until July 12, 2010, when the investigation ended.

Another law intended to "come to terms with history" was the Act for Identifying Truth of Anti-National and Pro-Japanese Acts under Japanese Colonial Occupation (February 13, 2004). This law was approved by virtually all members of the National Assembly, including members of the opposition Hannara Party.

Roh Moo-hyun was trying to come to terms with the history of both Japanese colonial rule and South Korean dictatorship at the same time. The democratization of Korea became the unifying theme that bundled them together. Thus emerged the political ideology of "pro-North equals anti-Japan equals Democracy," which took deep root in South Korean society, becoming a populist political movement.

Lee Myung-bak: "We have conquered Japan."

As previously discussed, Korea's civilian presidents have basically taken a forward-looking stance and maintained quiet diplomacy early in their term, turning against Japan only later when they faced a crisis. Lee Myung-bak (February 2008–February 2013) was no different. Warm toward Japan at the start, he stiffened his stance when opposition grew more outspoken. Still, he tried to keep an appropriate balance.

On August 10, 2011, the 100th anniversary of the Japan-Korea Annexation Treaty, the Japanese government issued an apology for the great harm that colonial rule had inflicted on the Korean people. In response, Korea's opposition parties, led by the Democratic Party, were dismissive: "[Japan] has simply repeated past statements."

On August 15 (Independence Day), President Lee Myung-bak took a more favorable tone, describing Japanese prime minister Naoto Kan's remarks as a step forward. "For the first time, Japan has reflected on its colonial rule, which transgressed the will of the Korean people, and apologized." South Korea's Democratic Party took Lee to task for falling for Japan's false apology. Within two weeks, Lee turned much more strongly against Japan.

At the end of August, Seoul's Chong-ro Ward, with the backing of the Lee government, approved the construction of a statue commemorating comfort women. The placement of the statue, directly across from the Japanese Embassy in Seoul, was deliberately provocative. The statue was commissioned by a support group for the comfort women, the Conference on Issues Regarding Korean Volunteer Corps, and endorsed by the minister of Health and Welfare. Bearing the title "Monument of Peace," the statue depicted a young girl sitting on a chair with another vacant chair beside her, symbolizing a comfort woman.

On August 31, President Lee Myung-bak said, in a televised interview:

"We are not worried about the rebuilding of North Korea; we will have Japan take care of it. I will make Japan pay for the entire project. That's because we have already conquered Japan. We have free use of their money." He continued, "Japan does not know anything. Fuji TV is the evidence. The Japanese people are drooling as they look at us. Leave it to me. In Japan I have highly trained soldiers who are faithful to my orders."

"The rumors spread by the Korea Democratic Party seem to be true. Starting in October this year, data on all Japanese residents will be processed on the Korean Peninsula because someone sold data containing private information on every Japanese."

The audio/video of this interview is available on YouTube.

In August, South Korea's Constitutional Court ruled that the government must press Japan to compensate private citizens in connection with the comfort women issue. On September 20, South Korea's Ministry of Trade, Industry, and Energy (MOTIE) proposed a meeting with Japan on the issue, but the Japanese government declined the invitation.

On September 20, a MOTIE press officer said President Lee Myung-bak and Japanese Prime Minister Yoshihiko Noda would discuss the issue of compensation for comfort women at a meeting in New York, but in fact their discussion did not broach the subject.

On October 11, the South Korea's representative raised the issue of comfort women at a meeting of the Third Committee of the UN General Assembly, asking the UN and its members to make efforts to "assist and compensate the victims of sex violence during the war." Japan countered by arguing that the matter of compensation had been settled by the 1951 San Francisco Peace Treaty and the 1965 Bilateral Agreement between Japan and Korea. South Korea argued, however, that the Japanese government still bore a legal obligation.

On December 14, the Monument of Peace was erected in front of the Japanese embassy in Seoul.

On June 16, 2012, a group of Korean residents in the United States erected a monument in Eisenhower Park, New York, to the comfort women, with an inscription saying the Japanese army forcibly mobilized more than 200,000 girls as sex slaves. "The Japanese Army's shameful crime should be acknowledged and must never be forgotten."

Landing on Takeshima (Dok-do), demand for emperor's apology

For some time, a private group in Seoul had been pressing for the erection of a memorial to the comfort women in front of the Japanese embassy. Initially, the Lee Myung-bak government tried to discourage this and showed restraint. Later, however, the government shifted its position, paving the way for the private sector to take the leading role in anti-Japan activity. At the same time, behind the scenes, the government tried to engage Japan in a dialogue on compensation for the former comfort women.

Truly shocking, however, was President Lee Myung-bak's interview with the TV station SBS. "We are not worried about the rebuilding of North Korea; we will have Japan take care of it. I will make Japan pay for the entire project." These remarks are the epitome of the smugness with which he had promised to implement his policy from the very beginning of his presidency.

In exchange for Pyongyang's abandonment of nuclear power development, he promised to increase North Korea's per capita income to $3,000. He said he would give $40 billion in aid to achieve this. And he said he would make Japan pay $10 billion of that aid.

Even more shocking was his vulgar insult: "We have already conquered Japan." Korean politicians tend to think that insulting Japan is the best way to win popular support.

It's almost as if Lee were saying something like this: "Japan these days has become deeply attached to Korean culture. Large Japanese corporations, media sponsors, advertising agencies, and

TV broadcasters are all flocking to Korean dramas, Korean music, and Korean stars. Fuji TV is typical. Japanese people just cannot get enough Korean culture. My policy of promoting Korean culture in Japan has been very successful. Japan is full of my 'soldiers' who have been mesmerized by my Japan policy. Leave the three major projects of the Korean people with me."

Lee's reaction to rumors spread by the Korean Democratic Party (Korean Socialist Democratic Party) had something to do with the fact that SoftBank Telecom Corp. won a bid to set up a large network for Japan's Ministry of Health, Labor, and Welfare involving a basic database for residents and postal services. It established a joint venture with Korea KT Corporation in South Korea as a data management center. NTT and KDDI had already established local companies in China and Korea, with local staff and Japanese management. SoftBank Telecom held a 51 percent stake in its joint venture in South Korea. Lee Myung-bak used these facts as the basis for his claim that someone in Japan had sold data on Japanese residents to Korea, and to bolster the notion of "conquering Japan with his own soldiers."

With this shift to a more stridently anti-Japan posture, public support for the government increased as the year entered into 2012. After the general election, however, with the arrests of people who were close to the president and his son, support for the government dropped sharply, to about 20 percent. Then Lee Myung-bak took another step to become even more strongly anti-Japan, traveling on August 10 to Takeshima (Dok-do) and making his notorious statement about the Japanese emperor.

"I was thinking about [my landing on Takeshima] for the

past few years. It was not a capricious act on my part, but rather a result of careful thinking. I also considered the side effects of opposing Japan. Because Japan does not fully understand the position of the aggressor and its victims, I was trying to awaken the Japanese."

If the Japanese emperor "wants to visit Korea, he should visit the graves of those who died fighting in the independence movement. He should *kneel* and express his heartfelt apology. Rather than worrying and searching for months for the right expression like 'painful and regretful feeling,' it would be better if he didn't visit Korea at all" (remarks at Korea Teachers College in Choong-chung Buk-do on August 14. The Office of the President omitted the word "kneel" from the Collection of President's Remarks; the italicized word was inserted by the author).

This unprecedentedly vulgar and insulting statement increased public support for the government from about 25 percent to 34 percent for a time. This was not to last, however, due to the many corruption incidents, the arrest of Lee's elder brother, and investigation of his son, as well as himself.

On December 12, 2012, North Korea launched a missile. A week later, a presidential election was held in South Korea amid a tense atmosphere of fear of an imminent nuclear test by North Korea (actually carried out in February 2013). In the election, Moon Jae-in of the Democratic Unification Party, associated with pro–North Korea elements, won 48 percent of the valid votes, just short of victory. This shows how much the ruling party maintained its influence.

Chapter IV

Why Can't the Anti-Japan Mentality Be Eradicated?

Anti-Japan nationalism and the falsification and fabrication of history

As we have seen, South Korea is a nation where anti-Japan ideology is deeply ingrained. What is the root cause for this? It is often said that the root cause is the historical fact of Japan's colonization of the Korean Peninsula in the first half of the 20th century. Surely, there would be no anti-Japan nationalism in Korea had there been no Japanese rule over the Korean Peninsula. That may be true, but it is not the same as saying that Japanese colonial rule shaped Korea's anti-Japan nationalism.

How, then, was it formed? It was formed in the postwar period through falsification and fabrication of the history of Japanese rule. In other words, Korea's anti-Japan nationalism was created not by the "truth" of historical experience, but rather by the "falsification and fabrication of history." Japan understands this but has failed to clearly point it out.

The first time Shinzo Abe was prime minister (September 26, 2006–September 26, 2007), he made statements regarding comfort women, which told the truth appropriately. Abe said consistently and repeatedly that he understands that these women felt they had to go with the military police even if they did not want to. There was an atmosphere of force in a broad sense, even if there was no force in a narrow sense of actually taking them from their homes. What Prime Minister Abe meant by "atmosphere of force in a broader sense" was the one inherent in the relationship between the ruler and the ruled, through due process consistent with modern law. "Force in a narrow sense" lacks due process.

In its rule over Korea, Japan exercised militaristic control in the early period, but this was later reformed, and there was a shift to civilized control. Japan extended its control to the entire range of daily life, with a pillar of modern reform based on use of force in a broader sense. It was basically not the case that the military police used "force in a narrow sense" openly against the general public. In all of world history of control of one country by another (colonial control), Japanese rule over Korea was exceptional. Regarding comfort women, the open use of "force in the narrow sense" was prohibited by the Japanese authorities, and it is a historical fact that it did not happen.

Those who personally experienced life during the period of Japanese rule are well aware of this historical fact. After World War II, however, Korean government bureaucrats and opportunistic intellectuals favored falsified and fabricated history, arguing that Japanese rule over Korea was based on open use of "force in a narrow sense," and of militaristic, violent, and plunderous control. These bureaucrats and intellectuals used this idea, alongside anti-Japan education, to convince the public that their falsified history was true.

After Japan's defeat in World War II, Korea embarked on the project of forging itself into a nation of citizens. In this process it felt a need to bring people together to create a unified national system. Korean leaders pushed the policy of making Japan the "enemy of the nation" for this purpose. They spread the policy throughout the country. Anti-Japan nationalism became the key to patriotism. Falsification and fabrication of history were essential elements in the execution of this policy.

How was it possible for Korea to create this falsified history? The answer to the question is a powerful ideological policy backed by the power of the state and the suppression of free speech.

In South Korea, the policy of anti-Japan nationalism took many forms. Still, based on common sense, it is not possible that force of authority alone could imbue an understanding of history so different from actual experience so deeply among the people of the nation. Nevertheless, the falsification and fabrication of history succeeded in South Korea. How did this happen?

National duty of informing against pro-Japan elements

South Korea is a democratic country as far as the system is concerned; so no matter how much control is exercised over information, or how strongly the anti-Japan policy is pushed, it is possible for people to freely gather a variety of information. Under normal circumstances, anti-Japan sentiment would be milder in South Korea than in China. In fact, though, anti-Japan senti-ment is stronger among Koreans than among Chinese people.

Of course, freedom of speech is suppressed in South Korea. Korean authorities barring my entry into the country is an exam-ple. Even so, the suppression of freedom of speech in South Korea is not as stiff as in China. South Korea is not a dictatorship. The anti-Japan ideology in South Korea today is one-dimensional. It can be inferred that the reason why anti-Japan ideology is so deep-rooted in South Korea has to do with factors other than the political regime in place. There must be something that allows people to accept this anti-Japan ideology. These factors have an impact on people. The strongest of these is that until very recently, historically speaking, the Korean Peninsula was ruled with an iron fist by an ancient dynasty.

Dictatorial control of the state means that power is centrally concentrated and emanates in all directions. Information can be controlled because people can be thoroughly and uniformly brainwashed. In such systems, top-down brainwashing is the norm, and people accept this as "wisdom from above." China has a vast territory, and its population is huge. This makes it more dif-ficult to enforce a uniform value system throughout the country, and so the state's control is incomplete. The Korean Peninsula is rather small, and so is the population. The state's control can be more complete than in China.

In Korea of the Joseon Dynasty, no one was ever allowed to violate the state's total control, even to the smallest degree. An important mechanism for enforcing that control was the nation-wide system of secret informants. People were required to report on anyone who expressed views counter to the policies of the state.

In South Korea today, there is a system to encourage people to report on other people who have committed crimes. Until the 1970s, it was common to see bulletin boards in towns and villages with official papers urging people to report to authorities anyone they suspect of being pro-Japan or pro–North Korea. There were rewards for making such reports and penalties for failing to do so.

For example, if there was someone who could speak Japanese, the person had to be reported. In fact, when I was younger, there was someone in my neighborhood who spoke Japanese; people thought the person suspicious, and someone reported on the person. It turned out that the person was actually Japanese, so that was the end of it. But people who could speak Japanese had to be extremely cautious. I have heard stories about people who were reported by their own family members.

Many people who experienced Japanese rule were pro-Japan

In South Korea today, many people who are now 75 years old or older experienced life under Japanese rule, and many of them have a favorable view of Japan. When I was a child, my parents and their contemporaries often told me that Japanese people were very kind. At school, however, I was taught that Japan had done horrible things to Korean people. As a result, people younger than about 70 years old, educated in the postwar, anti-Japan system, have all been brainwashed, and it is understandable that they are anti-Japan.

I have interviewed many Japanese and Koreans who experienced life in Korea under Japanese rule, and I discussed the life stories of 10 Japanese and 5 Koreans in the book *People's Lives During the Japanese Period of Rule* (Sankosha). The Japanese people I profiled all said they had gotten along well with their Korean neighbors, and most of the Koreans said the same of the Japanese. No one spoke of discrimination of any kind.

The only available research I am aware of regarding people's attitudes on this subject was conducted by Korean anthropologist Choi Gil-seong, who was a professor at Japanese universities. He published his research on "Pro-Japan and Anti-Japan Consciousness of Residents in Koumun-do in Korea" (research period, November 1, 1987–January 10, 1988). According to this paper, older people were more pro-Japan, and younger people were more anti-Japan. Analyzing his research, Choi Gil-seong said:

"I came to realize that, while the people who experienced life (during the period of Japanese rule) showed positive attitudes toward Japan, those in the young generation, who never experienced this, showed negative attitudes toward Japan. This result reflected the fact that people in the postwar generation received (anti-Japan) ideological education.

"Colonial control in villages is a matter of degree. It was often thought that (Japanese control) was better than the cruel Joseon dynasty, which employed the *yangban* system, and the postwar dictatorships. Korean scholars biased toward democracy tend to focus on the independence movement against the policy of aggression. As nationalism heightened, this tendency became more pronounced, due to the polarization of ideology. As a result, most results of their research presented the negative side [of Japanese rule], but lacked objectivity. Research results became increasingly divorced from the general public. In short, at the village level, there are people who saw colonial rule affirmatively. This is what we learned from interviews with people who experienced life under Japanese rule." (Choi Gil-seong, *Japanese Colony and Changes in Culture: Komoon-do Korea* [published by Ochanomizu shobo, 1988])

One thing is clear. In the more than 60 years that have passed since the end of World War II, South Korea has steadfastly continued its strong anti-Japan education, and this has shaped Korea's anti-Japan nationalism.

South Korea tolerates just One view of history

South Korea's anti-Japan education has many aspects. Consider the example of land issues.

The colonial-era Japanese Government-General surveyed the land of South Korea to determine its area, ownership, and usage to help in its task of governing. What Korean students have been taught is different from these historical facts. The textbooks that I myself used as a child in South Korea, as well as those currently in use, begin with the phrase, "Imperial Japan, in order to loot the land...." Students are misled to learn that Imperial Japan's primary intention was to loot the land from the Korean people. From a more objective historical standpoint, however, it is clear that the Japanese colonial government had a basic policy aim of modernizing the administration of land ownership and conducted the land survey for this purpose. The Korean teaching, that the project's aim was "to loot the land," shapes the work of historians and researchers who were educated in this system.

Korean students are all taught one view of history. They are prohibited from learning any other views. Students are educated to evaluate history, its characteristics, development, etc. without stepping away from that one prescribed viewpoint.

If they start from the premise that Imperial Japan's main aim was to loot the land, then the wresting of the land from the people was an act of unspeakable cruelty. According to documents from the Japanese colonial administration, however, "the Japanese Government-General of Korea requisitioned only 3 percent of all farmland [discussed in detail later in chapter V]. The figure of 3 percent is too low to be described as "cruel." For this reason, South Korean textbooks omit this figure. If they were to mention it, their singular historical viewpoint would collapse, and their lies would be exposed. In fact, however, the figure was 3 percent.

The figure used in South Korean textbooks is that "40 percent of farmland was looted." This figure, however, is not based on any scientific and academic foundation. It is used only to establish consistency with the assertion that Imperial Japan looted the land. Absolutely no reference is given to the source of this figure or how it was derived.

The Korean race: One big interrelated group

This view of history may be rooted in racial identity in Korea. Among the nations of the world, Japan and Korea are unique. They are the only countries where, for over 1,000 years, racial identity and the nation-state have been virtually the same. While they are alike in this characteristic, Japan and Korea are very different from one another in how people think about and sense the concept of race.

In the early history of Japan, farm villages sprang up that were communities unrelated to blood lineage. These communities had a system based on both paternal and maternal lineage, aimed at the continuation of the household lineage, not that of blood lineage. In Korea, on the other hand, as in many Asian countries, the formation of farming villages was based on blood lineage. Korea attaches much greater importance to blood lineage than is the case in, say, China or Taiwan. Traditionally, Korean society is based on the continuation of paternal lineage.

"*Jongjok*" is the term used in Korea for paternal lineage. The same characters as those for jongjok, but with different pronunciation, are also used in China (and Japan) to mean the same thing. Korea's conceptualization of the nation-state is no more than an expanded version of *jongjok*, one big family based on paternal lineage. The king sat at the apex of the nation, and in Korea from ancient times the king was known as "Father of the Nation," and the king's legal wife was the "Mother of the Nation." In North Korea, Kim Il-sung was called "Father of the Nation," and the term persisted in South Korea until the presidency of Chun

Doo-hwan. In other words, the moral and ethical principles were the same at all levels: family, society, and nation-state. This tradition is rooted in Confucianism. For Koreans, both North and South, racial identity is a matter of one big blood-related community.

In the modern sense, racial identity is a regional community that shares a language and culture. No matter how large the region is, race does not refer to blood lineage. In South Korea, however, racial identity refers to blood-lineage. South Koreans' concept of race is nothing more than a geographically expanded version of their traditional society of blood relatives.

Ideology: Japanese are inferior, Koreans are superior

Korea's racism against Japan is rooted in its history of looking down on Japan. The antipathy toward Japan so often expressed in Korea is not based on the history of Japanese colonization. Koreans find it intolerable that they were conquered by a race they see as contemptible. That is why they are so vehement in their antipathy toward Japan.

Koreans' antipathy toward Japan is based on a bias that Japanese people are "born barbarians who are aggressive by nature." This idea stems from a historical view of the Japan-Korea relations, as discussed below.

In ancient times when Japan had no culture to speak of, Korea gave it Confucianism, Buddhism, technology, and other high-level cultural assets. Japan, however, forgot about the favors it received from Korea. Instead, its history books record fabricated narratives that Empress Jingu conquered the three kingdoms of Korea around the year 200 a.d., and of a Mimana Japan state in ancient times. Historically speaking, in the medieval era, Toyotomi Hideyoshi invaded Korea. By the mid-19th century, Japanese scholars had concocted a rationale that led to the 1875 Ganghwa Island Incident. Then at the end of the Meiji period, Japan annexed Korea and began its 36 years of control over Korea.

By putting these disparate elements together in a single, continuous narrative, Koreans feel justified in seeing the Japanese as "barbarians who are aggressive by nature," and that is the basis of Korean antipathy toward Japan.

How do Koreans make the leap from antipathy to disdain? Throughout history, the various nations that have ruled the Korean Peninsula have always disdained Japan because China was the center, the benevolent power that ordered their world, and Japan was further on the periphery of that world.

In this ancient order of the Asian world, China was the center of all cultures, and other nations were peripheral, barbarian nations to be subjugated and/or invaded. This was the basic world view of the China-centered world order. For over 1,000 years, China was the center of this world, the various nations that have occupied the Korean Peninsula were its loyal subjects, and both viewed Japan as a barbarian nation to be influenced, subjugated, and even invaded. This historical mindset is at the root of Korea's contemporary antipathy toward Japan.

Confucianism teaches that people in a superior position in the moral order must influence, educate, and discipline those beneath them, and this tenet also has shaped Korea's traditional disdain for Japan. This idea is behind Koreans' belief in their own racial superiority over Japan. Koreans pridefully believe they are rightful successors of the China-centered world order. Sinocentrism is a form of hidden ethnocentrism. This only reinforces Koreans' sense of their own superiority vis-à-vis Japan. Korean antipathy toward Japan is, above all, an expression of revulsion at the notion that Japanese people, upon whom "we" bestowed culture, who are "beneath us," should "look down upon us" and "make fools of us," in the Takeshima (Dok-Do) territorial dispute, the visits to Yasukuni Shrine, the comfort women issue, and so on.

As can be seen in many Asian and African countries that became independent after World War II, racism takes ethnocentrism as its point of departure. This is not unlike the "white superiority" thinking that was common in Western nations in the past. Whether to a greater or lesser extent, what nation-states that are based on race share is that they are based on ethnocentrism, a belief that their race is superior to others. Whether kept private or made public, some degree of a sense of superiority was essential in the early period of the establishment of racism.

Racism in South Korea has not advanced even one step forward from that stage, and the reason is that South Korea's racism is founded on its anti-Japan ideology. Without anti-Japan ideology, Koreans would have no reason to think their own race was superior to others. Anti-Japan ideology lies at the very core of the conception of South Korea as a nation-state. There is no other nation like South Korea.

History of continuous disdain for Japanese people

From historical documents it is clear that Korea (the various nations that have ruled the Korean Peninsula over the centuries) disdained Japan even before modern times. In 1719 (fourth year of the Kyoho period), a group of Korean emissaries visited Japan. Among them was Shin Yu-han, a scribe (bureaucrat), who wrote down what was told to him by Amenomori Hoshu, a samurai from the Tsushima clan:

"Japan and your country across the sea are a pair of neighboring countries. The trust between us is unchanging. … However, in my private reading of a collection of writings from your country, the references to Japan always regard us as a country of uneducated people and barbarians. I feel ashamed and astounded, and cannot accept this.… I wonder whether you are aware of this.… Even now your delegation always calls us 'uneducated people.' …

This is not what we wish." (Shin Yu-han, *Kaiyuroku* [Record of Travel Overseas], [Tokyo: Heibonsha, 2003] translated from Korean by Kan jae-oun.)

Amenomori Hoshu asked Shin Yu-han why Koreans have looked down on Japanese since ancient times and why Koreans continued to disdain Japanese. Shin Yu-han responded, "That reference must have been written after the Imjin War (Toyotomi Hideyoshi's invasion of Korea)." He added, "Hideyoshi is our country's ultimate foe. There is no Korean who does not dream of chopping up his flesh and eating it." Shin Yu-Han felt no shame in saying it was all right for Koreans to disdain Japanese because Toyotomi Hideyoshi had invaded Korea. It was a complete falsehood, however, to say that Korea's disdain for Japan began with the Imjin War.

With the exception of formal, national documents, since ancient times the various nations that have existed on the Korean Peninsula have consistently written condescendingly of Japan, calling it a nation of uneducated people or barbarians, or even more disdainful expressions. The Joseon Dynasty was no exception.

These exchanges between Amenomori Hoshu and Shin Yu-han would be little different today.

During the anti-Japanese demonstrations, South Koreans were openly disdainful, burning Japanese flags and stamping on pictures of the prime minister. Major South Korean newspapers used unbearably disdainful words like "extreme rightist" for the democratically elected Prime Minister Abe. If Japanese people object and say such expressions are unwarranted, South Koreans respond that Japan invaded Korea and made Koreans suffer. Nothing has changed since the days of Shin Yu-han.

Sense of humiliation directly impacts people's physiology

South Korea's government leaders and intellectuals have fabricated a mythology that they want the public to believe, that "the Japanese race are born barbarians and aggressive by nature," who "insulted the sacred unity of our race's blood lineage." "Unity of blood" means the unity of a community of blood relatives sharing a common destiny, bound by the same singular blood, a code phrase signifying that race (homogeneous race) is just an expanded version of a family or extended family, based on blood lineage. "Unity of blood" is a sacred thing, signifying that, in ethical terms, the same justice and benevolence one extends to one's relatives should also be extended to one's entire race.

Because South Koreans' sense of race is based on blood bonds rather than common culture, their antipathy toward Japanese people has a strong physiological dimension. Speaking from my own experience of antipathy to Japan, when I was young my parents and others of their generation told stories about land being taken and Japanese-language education forced upon them. People who fought for independence were killed, tortured, and taken away by force. Whenever I heard such stories, I felt an unspeakable humiliation, as if I myself had been defiled, with the ensuing conviction that I could never forgive such things, nor could I let go of my own rancor. My anger was practically a physiological reaction.

Anti-Japan activists in South Korea showed no hesitation in jumping onto the stories they heard from anti-Japan activists in Japan about the comfort women, even though such stories had previously been unknown in South Korea. They believed the stories, without fact-checking them; they fit their mythology that Japanese people are "born barbarians with aggressive natures who have humiliated the sacred blood unity of the race." The fact that these stories were about sex also gave them an especially strong sense of humiliation because it tied in to the physiological dimension of anti-Japan sentiment.

For South Koreans, the comfort women issue is a matter of direct, physiological assault on the "sacred blood unity of the Korean race." These were incidents that sullied the blood of the Korean race, a tremendous emotional assault on the Korean race.

The sense or principle that the "unity of the blood of the Korean race" was sacred is not something that began after World War II. It dates back to the mid-19th century, when the Meiji Restoration was happening in Japan, allowing the Joseon Dynasty in Korea to resume relations with its island neighbor.

Starting around the time of the Meiji Restoration, as a matter of national policy, the Joseon Dynasty prohibited Korean women from engaging in sexual relations with Japanese men. The penalty for the violators was beheading, and local officials in charge could lose their jobs. This policy was established mainly to discourage relations between Korean women and Japanese men in Busan, where some contact between Japan and Korea continued even during the Edo period.

Around 1876, when the Japan-Korea Friendship Treaty was signed, the Joseon Dynasty faced years of poor crops, which resulted in many deaths from hunger. Women from poor farm families secretly came to the "Japanese Houses" in Busan and sold sex to get food.

Many of the Japanese who bought sex from these women were sailors or merchants. Many Korean women were arrested and punished. Japanese newspapers during the period reported the following:

"The heads of the towns of Dongre, Busan and Suyeong came and decreed the executions. The women were bound with coarse ropes, and the openings of their ears were pierced by small, white-fletched arrows. They were stretched on their backs with their heads on wooden pillows. Blades like hatchets were laid across their necks, for the executioners to strike with wooden hammers to chop off their heads. As one woman was brought to the execution site, she quietly took in the scene and said, 'I had no other future than to die of hunger. With the help of the Japanese I was able to live another 40–50 days. Today, I will escape the sufferings of hunger,' with tears streaming down her face" (summarized from an article in a Japanese newspaper, *Hochi Shimbun*, October 2, 1877).

Why was it a capital crime for Korean women to have sex with Japanese men? The reason was that Koreans thought of Japanese as contemptible barbarians historically worthy of scorn. Such barbarians must not be allowed to violate women who were royal subjects of Korea. This was the real reason for the policy of national prohibition.

With respect to the 20th-century issue of comfort women as well, undeniably there is a psychological dimension that strongly contributes, whether consciously or unconsciously, to Koreans' ill feelings of having been "racially humiliated by (Japanese) barbarians."

Essence of the World War II comfort women issue

Historically, in farming villages in poor Asian countries, whenever famine strikes or when the nation suffers from war or civil strife, or in areas suffering unending extreme poverty, women have sold sex to survive. This history has continued for millennia. That this situation continues even now is shown by the countless women standing on street corners in cities across Asia, and by the many women from Asian countries who come to Japan to work.

Needless to say, selling sex allows them to earn money and support themselves and their families. It is not just that they want to get money for their private life. Even in the present day, there are many reasons for women to choose this option (or have it thrust upon them). They may support a family because the father is sick, or an older or younger brother needs to go to school. There were even young women who went from Japan to the Chinese mainland to earn money. Historically, poverty has forced women across Asia to do what they have to do.

This is the context in which the issue of the comfort women should be viewed.

The battlefield is not a normal environment, and if soldiers are unable to satisfy their sexual needs, social disruption may result. This is a matter of historical experience. Discussions about comfort women tend to overlook these truths.

Koreans who experienced what it meant to be so-called comfort women all went to the front lines of war knowing that, in the impoverished conditions of war-torn Asia, this was the only way they could go on living, for their families. The misery they tasted in life was not that they were cheated by pimps or sold by their parents or used for the amusement of soldiers. They suffered because they had no one to blame but themselves.

In traditional Korean society, it was a woman's duty to bear descendants of the paternal lineage. Women had to bear sons no matter what, and they were to preserve their virtue to the death (not to sully the blood of paternal lineage). This was the strong, Confucian moral code of Korean society at the time of the comfort women.

In the context of the moral code that existed in traditional Korean society, to be a comfort woman was to be a criminal who violated the fundamental ethics of human beings. The suffering of these women's lives is that they have continued to blame themselves as criminals, tortured by the sense that they committed serious crimes.

In the extreme conditions of Asian poverty, when very normal women resolve to live on their own strength, together with their family, they inevitably face the issue of sex. The issue of the comfort women is a sharp reminder of the history of both the past and the present conditions in impoverished, agricultural Asia.

No one ever witnessed a Korean woman being forced into sex slavery

Unfortunately, none of the testimonies given by women who experienced what it was to be a comfort woman can be said to be honest about their circumstances or their true feelings.

Because these women were Koreans, even if it was true that their parents had sold them or Korean pimps had cheated them, they were well aware that revealing these facts would benefit Imperial Japan. They knew this would mean they would be shunned by society, even more than before.

Anti-Japan activists asked them, "Isn't it true you were taken away by force?" and the form of this question offered them an unexpected way out. For the first time, they were able to connect with ordinary people in a way they had not anticipated. Until that point, society had looked coldly on them, and they thought they had done something for which they had only themselves to blame. Suddenly they realized they could be saved if they said they had been "forced." Sad to say, but they were simply clutching at the words of the anti-Japan activists. At least that's what I think.

On the evening of September 2, 2004, there was a TV program called "MBC 100 Minutes Debate." The theme of the program was "Investigating the Truth of Past Events." During the discussion, Lee Young-hoon, a professor of economics at Seoul National University, said, "Show me one Korean scholar who thinks the Government-General of Korea forcibly mobilized comfort women. (I don't know of any.)" This caused quite a ruckus, and Lee received many stronglyworded protests, some demanding that he resign his professorship. In the end, he was only able to quiet the fuss by going to see some former comfort women and offering an abject, prostrate apology.

As long as Korean people believe the myth that Japanese people are "born barbarians, aggressive by nature, who insulted the sacred unity of our race's blood lineage," they must also believe there was "use of force in a narrow sense" without ever investigating the truth.

That is the real issue. Historically, government administrators in Korea had a tradition of ignoring poverty in rural villages, but the activists who dwell on the comfort women issue never call that a problem. Instead, they try to shift the blame to Japanese militarism. Similarly, do-gooders in advanced countries, who show their sympathy by bandying about the word "sex slaves," are no better.

I was born in South Korea and lived there until I was 26. I never heard any story about soldiers or officials of the Japanese Government-General forcibly removing village women from their homes. Of the people I interviewed for my book *People's Lives During the Japanese Period of Rule* (Sankosha) not a single person said he or she had seen or heard of anything like that.

It is ridiculous that such stories have emerged only recently. Only since Japanese leftists contacted Korean anti-Japan nationalists has this story escalated from "something like that might have happened," to "something like that must have happened," and further to "something like that in fact happened."

The comfort women story has been deliberately conflated with the story about women draftees, creating a story that a large number of women were forcibly removed from their homes to become comfort women. This story has come to be accepted in Korea as reality.

In Korea today, prostitutes call out from behind glass windows to men passing on the street. Prostitution is illegal in Korea, but it is brazenly practiced. Many young girls work as prostitutes. When I researched the subject around 1990, I learned that many of these prostitutes were sold by their parents, or they were divorced and could not return to their homes, or they had been abducted. There are still places where this is true.

South Korea has demanded that history textbooks in Japan deal with the issue of comfort women. I concur. As I have discussed here, Japan should make it clear that this is a problem stemming from rural poverty in Asia and the sexual needs of soldiers at war. Every time I think about the absence of such a discussion, I have to grumble to myself about "do-gooders in advanced countries."

Reasons for absence of a global view of history

Generally speaking, in South Korea, Japan's colonial domination of Korea is viewed as a hardship that was visited upon Korean people alone. There is practically zero understanding of colonization as a recurring theme in human history throughout the world. For this reason, Koreans—and this was true of myself as well—do not even try to place the matter of Japanese rule over Korea in the proper context of world history.

I first came to question South Korea's understanding of history after I came to Japan. I began to read every book I could get my hands on about Japan-Korea relations, from early-modern times to the present. I am still learning. I have tried to set aside the Korean view of history and, with the help of writings by Japanese and Western scholars, to bring some light to bear on the situation under which Japan was operating. The narrative of historical developments I have come to accept goes something like this:

(1) After opening its own borders during the Meiji Restoration, Japan asked Korea several times to open up its borders, but Korea stubbornly refused. This caused Japan to see portents of a major crisis in Korea. Japan reasoned that Korea had to move quickly to become more open, modernize, and become more wealthy, with a stronger military, or else it would face the risk of coming under the control of the Western powers. If that happened, then Japan, as Korea's neighbor, would be in a predicament.

(2) Amid this tense situation in world affairs, the view emerged in Japan that it would have to open Korea by force. This was the "Policy of conquering Korea by military force" in the early part of the Meiji Era.

(3) The aim of the "Policy of conquering Korea by military force" was not merely to invade Korea. It was to destroy the sinocentric East Asian world order. Japan intended to oust China from the center of the East Asian world order that had prevailed since ancient times, and to create a new East Asian world order with its own hands, fighting back against the invasion of Asia by the Western powers. Its first step was to separate Korea from this world order. The first order of diplomatic business for modern Japan was Korea's independence from the grip of China.

(4) Korea's independence was accomplished through Japan's

victory in the Sino-Japanese War (1894-95). However, Korea proved unable to lead itself to raise the banner of its own independence. Korea started to modernize, but it maintained a pro-China government that advocated the idea of subjugation to China.

(5) In the period after the Sino-Japanese War, Korea also cozied up to Russia with the idea of obtaining its protection, but Korea came under Japan's protection after the Russo-Japanese War (1904-05).

(6) Throughout this period, Korea remained unable to assert its independence and remained under the sway of Imperial China. When Korea realized that China did not have Korea's interests at heart, it tried to ally with the other Asian giant, Russia. Korea did not want to align itself with Japan, which it still regarded as a small and barbarian nation.

This timeline of historical events, up to Japan's annexation of Korea, has caused me to think deeply about why Korea could not assert its own independence. What exactly led to the annexation? I have come to realize that Korea itself thinks the main factor was simply the government corruption of the Joseon Dynasty, but it has failed to reflect on what other domestic factors may have contributed.

After reading materials in Japan, I came to realize:

- Western scholars writing on the period of Japan's control over Korea severely criticize the terrible political corruption of the Joseon Dynasty.

- Most of these writers argue that Japan's control over Korea was the result of a natural series of international events, and they say that Japan generally practiced good governance.

- A significant number of Japanese, European, and American writers view the time leading up to World War II as a period of imperialism and colonialism generally. A clash occurred between Japanese imperialism on the one hand and Western imperialism on the other. They are critical of European and American countries as well as Japan.

- Some Europeans and Americans concede that the war with Japan played a role in liberating Asian countries from colonialism.

When I was in Korea, I never realized there are so many different ways of thinking about this history. I thought about Japan's colonial rule only as a misfortune that befell the Korean people. I came to understand, however, that most of the books I read in Japan were written from a broader perspective of world history. Many of these books had not been translated into the Korean language and were not available in South Korea.

Korea's anti-Japan nationalists continued to insist that Japanese were "barbarian and aggressive," and that Koreans should continue to harangue them about crimes they committed until the Japanese apologize and provide compensation for their crimes.

When I told this to Japanese people, they would often respond that they could not believe that such an outmoded view of the world, morality, and history still existed. Throughout its history, until very recently, Korea had always been ruled by either a king or a dictator. Thus, it was difficult for modern ways of thinking to take hold.

Chapter V

How Did Japan Rule Over Korea?

Differences between Western colonization and Japan's rule over Korea

fter the signing of the Japan-Korea Annexation Treaty on August 22, 1910, the Joseon Dynasty disappeared and the Korean Peninsula came under the control of Japan. This has generally been described as the colonization of the Korean Peninsula by Japan. Whatever the objectives of colonization, it can be said generally that any territory that is subject to another country is a colony of that country if the legal framework is different and the mother country's constitution and other laws and rules are not applied in their entirety. Korea under Japan's control was clearly a colony of Japan in the sense that it was Japanese territory under the law. Nonetheless, Japan's rule over Korea was very different from Western powers' control over their colonies.

(1) Japan implemented no policies aimed at exploiting Korea.

(2) Japan did not use armed suppression to govern.

(3) Japan rigorously promoted the modernization of culture, society, and education.

(4) Japan promoted the assimilation of Korean people into mainland Japan.

By contrast, Western powers benefited by exploiting the assets of their colonies. They controlled the territory with armed suppression. They did not modernize culture, society, and education. And they did not aim to assimilate the people of the colony into the mainland. For Western powers, colonial control remained a matter of controlling a foreign nation, not making it an integral part of their own nation.

The Western powers showed no hesitation in using suppression and murder to deal with resistance to their colonial control in Asian countries. The Netherlands carried out brutal suppression in Indonesia, as did Britain in India and France in Vietnam. There were massacres in these colonies that were intentional revenge against resistance activities, used as merciless lessons and not the result of overzealous suppression of riots such as the 3.1 Independence Movement in Korea. When the United States invaded the Philippines, its military forces murdered hundreds of thousands. In 1906, for example, they murdered 600 people, both soldiers and unarmed civilians, young and old, men and women, who had taken refuge in a fort after riots erupted to protest the land ownership system.

Western powers did not develop local industries as Japan did by directly investing huge amounts of capital. Western powers basically plundered raw materials from the colonies, benefiting their homelands. What about Japan? While Japan managed to show a surplus with its colony Taiwan, it continued until the end to show deficits in Manchuria and Korea. Most investment by Western powers in their colonies took the form of financial assets that could be repatriated at a moment's notice. Not one of the Western powers developed culture and education in their colonies the way Japan did.

Despite harsh control, there was no strong anti-Dutch nationalism in Indonesia, anti-British nationalism in India, or anti-French nationalism in Vietnam that could compare with the strength of anti-Japan nationalism in Korea. And in no former Western colony in Asia can we see the kind of grudge against the former colonial master that Korea shows toward Japan.

Western powers made great efforts to spread Christianity in their colonies, but none of them constructed public or private schools the way Japan did in Korea. The United States is said to have spread modern education, but not on the same scale as Japan. The Western powers did not promote modern education in their colonies. Instead, their main education policy was to send the children of senior officials in the colonies to schools in the mother country. The Netherlands provided no modern education at all for local people. It even prohibited the teaching of the Dutch language.

For Western powers, colonies were nothing but a place to exploit for their own benefit. If that is the case, it is wrong to describe Korea as Japan's "colony." This is the most important point in considering Japan's control over Korea.

Did living standards in Korea improve under Japanese rule?

Korea criticizes Japan for looting a great amount of wealth, pursuing profits, and stamping out Korea's own culture. At the same time, Korea gives Japan no credit at all for raising living standards and education, or for modernizing industry and transportation or instituting social reforms.

In discussing colonization, whether by Western nations or Japan, it is very common for people to talk only about damages while overlooking benefits. It is common to say colonization is bad and liberation is good. This ethical posture has taken firm root since World War II.

Those who simply think colonialism is evil have, consciously or unconsciously, internalized ideas that started with Vladimir Lenin's thoughts on war against imperialism. Lenin said that when one country invades another and places on it its own control, that is an imperialist war. Russian Marxists call colonization an invasion even if no war is waged on foreign soil. They regard it as an imperialist war, morally wrong, and a criminal act. This is essentially the same as the Korean view. Korea's anti-Japan nationalists hold the Leninist view of imperialist war close to their hearts, and use it as a stick with which to beat Japan.

For the common people of Korea, however, it is quite possible that life under Japanese control was much better than either before or after. Many people believe that the post-liberation Korean government was more tyrannical than the Japanese colonial administration.

Without looking at the specifics of the situation, some people seem to think they need to stand on a principle of self-determination as a moral value of the highest order. No matter how benevolent a colonial power may be, they judge any control over another country as a form of plunder that benefits only the colonial power. This idea is clearly wrong.

The equation of colonialism with evil leaves no room for credit if people's standard of living actually improved. People who think colonialism is a priori evil often speak in terms of "carrots" and "sticks." If they see any sign of a stick, they are quick to cherry-pick the details supporting their argument that colonialism is evil, and then they exaggerate them out of proportion. Over time, people come to accept such specious argumentation as fact. In Korea, where the post–World War generation is now the majority, such thinking is more prevalent than ever before. It is quite prevalent in Japan as well.

This is absurd. Under colonial control, good things happened as well as bad things. There were benefits as well as harm. This is the unvarnished truth. People who hear me say this often criticize me, accusing me of being an apologist for colonialism or an unreconstructed fan of imperialism. In South Korea it gets even worse. People call me a traitor to my race. In fact, my case is part of this story.

In any discussion of colonialism, the most important question has to be whether the colonial government infringed on the lives of the common people. All other questions are secondary. What does this mean? The important questions that most people want answers for deal with whether the colonial power harmed the lives of ordinary people in the colony: whether they plundered property, inflicted violence, raped women, or abducted people.

As far as I have been able to learn, Japan basically did not do things like that in Korea. I have interviewed many Koreans of the wartime generation, but none spoke of any personal experience of such atrocious acts. The only occasions on which I heard about atrocities were either rumors or hearsay whose veracity could not be ascertained.

Japanese rule as seen by people who experienced it

The necessary precondition for seeing that there were good aspects to life during the colonial period is the actual experience of the overall life of the vast majority of people: their daily lives under colonial rule were not significantly violated or disturbed; they had sad times and bad times, but this would have happened anyway. In all honesty, people do not care if their rulers are domestic or foreign, as long as their daily lives are not disturbed.

There is no one in this world who would prefer tyrannical control by a government of their own people over benevolent rule by a colonial power. Government by a foreign race is not inherently evil, any more than domestic rule is inherently good. If government violates the peace and security of the community, that government is bad, whether it is foreign or domestic.

What I have learned from the experience and the history of the generation before me is that, if the government tries to violate the lives of ordinary people, the people band together and fight back. Any serious violation of everyday life is a matter of life and death for the people of any country, and they will fight back resolutely, whether they are contending with a colonial government or not.

Setting aside questions of good and evil, we must see the flow of history for what it is. What impact did colonial rule have on the lives of ordinary people? What were the physical and psychological aspects? There is no room for doubt that this is the approach we must take, whether we are talking about a foreign ruler or a domestic government. Last but not least, we must examine dispassionately the reasons, both foreign and domestic, why the principle of self-rule failed.

The question of colonialism should not be weighed on the moral scale of good and evil. The key issue is how ordinary people were able to live under the political parameters prevailing at the time. Japanese rule abolished the tyrannical control of the Joseon Dynasty and established rule of law. As a result, life improved under Japanese rule, so much that there was no comparison to what had gone before.

By the same token, we should attach no special moral significance to Korea's liberation from its colonial rulers. Kim Il-sung in the North and Rhee Syng-man in the South were not strict practitioners of the rule of law. They were despots who trampled on human rights. This, too, we must examine very seriously.

Regrettably, we must come to the conclusion that the period of Japanese control was the "good times," when ordinary people's lives were incomparably better than in the times both before and after.

Shift from military rule to civilian rule

The 3.1 Independence Movement, which came to a head in the ninth year of Japanese rule (1919), marked a clear line of change. The Japanese Government-General learned that the implementation of its policies had fanned the flames of the independence movement. In response to the demands of the independence movement, the government speedily reformed the legal system within the framework of military rule. The main elements of this reform included paving the way for civilians to become governor, removing local control of the military from the hands of the governor, and introducing a civilian police force. The last of these was the most important. The security of the people improved significantly, and the number of arrests dropped sharply.

The government abolished restrictions on freedom of speech, press, assembly, and formation of companies. From this time, Japan ended its suppressive control over Korea and adopted systems as close as possible, though not identical, to those in place in Japan. Through these reforms, the government did away with uniforms for officials and teachers and ended the practice of carrying swords. Until that point, even schoolteachers wore sheathed swords in their belts and uniforms with golden epaulets. These two changes in particular had a tremendous impact on ordinary people, who found the teachers' prior appearance frightening.

Korean textbooks make no reference to these reforms. They are written as if Japanese rule remained the same from beginning to end. From that time forward, both the government and the private sector made great strides in ending discrimination. Still, differences in pay persisted, because "expatriate allowances" for Japanese nationals remained in place until the end of Japanese rule.

I have been surprised to learn that even Japanese people think Japan must have put in place a strong system of military control throughout Korea and suppressed popular resistance through oppressive governance. The opposite is true. Generally speaking, Japanese rule was not military control, or suppression, or oppression. From the very earliest years, the Government-General tried to shift from military government to civilian government. This is why there were no large-scale riots or popular resistance against Japanese rule in Korea after the 3.1 Independence Movement.

In its colonial rule over Korea, Japan's policy was to shift gradually to the same legal system it had at home. There were no elections in Korea under Japanese rule, but Koreans residing in Japan could vote. In 1945, the Government-General revised the election law in Korea, making residents of the Korean Peninsula eligible to vote and to run for office. However, Japan was defeated in the war shortly after this reform, and it never materialized.

Land reform in Korea under Japanese rule

The Government-General of Korea earnestly promoted the modern land survey. This project made it possible for the first time to construct modern infrastructure for transportation, communications, and expansion of farmland. Modern factories and hydroelectric plants were built throughout Korea. Large industrial parks were opened, and commercial business flourished.

From September 1910 through November 1918, the land survey compiled a register of land ownership (titles, deeds, plans), at a cost of 24.56 million yen. This project was similar to Japan's Land-Tax Reform of 1873.

The land survey recorded the ownership, value, topography, and other features of the land. The four main purposes of the project were:

(1) Establishment of a modern land-ownership system based on publicly approved ownership.

(2) Elimination of traditional disputes regarding ownership.

(3) Establishment of a land tax matched to modern production capacity.

(4) Establishment of a fair land-tax burden.

Korea had never known a modern regime, and the system of land ownership was murky. Under the Joseon Dynasty, Korea had a caste system, and it was common for the "Yangban" nobles to take land violently. Farmers engaged in endless disputes over land ownership. The feudal bureaucracy did not have a firm grip on the country's topography.

The Japanese colonial administration established a temporary bureau of land survey in September 1910, one month after the annexation. In 1912, it established a High Commission and began the full-bore land survey of Korea. The project was completed in November 1918 and established ownership of land, with the exception of forests, where the survey went on until 1922. The total certified land area of Korea was 4.42 million *jung-bo* (about 11 million acres) at the end of 1918. Of this total, 3.91 million *jung-bo* was owned by Koreans, 0.27 million *jung-bo* was owned by the nation, and 0.24 million *jung-bo* was owned by Japanese. The Government-General of Korea claimed 0.12 million *jung-bo* that was determined to be public land because its ownership was unclear. In addition, the government claimed 27,000 *jung-bo* for which ownership was unknown. Thus, the land taken by the Government-General of Korea was about 3 percent of the total.

On the subject of the land survey, Korean middle school history textbooks (approved by the national government) have this to say:

"To plunder the land, Imperial Japan made the excuse of clarifying land ownership in a modern way and made farmers register their land. The farmers, however, found this registration bothersome, and many resisted the Imperial order. As a result, many failed to register. The land that was not registered was regarded as ownerless, and it became the property of the Government-General.

"Many plots of land that had belonged to the Joseon emperor and Korean public institutions also became Government-General possessions. In addition, many parcels of land belonging to extended family units and regional communities were confiscated. A vast area equivalent to about 40 percent of all farmland in Korea was occupied by the Government-General, which in turn sold the land cheaply to Japanese land companies such as Toyo Takushoku Company or to Japanese immigrants" (quotation from 2002 Korean textbook). This content is unchanged even now.

The assertion that the Government-General confiscated 40 percent of the farmland in Korea cannot be reconciled with the historical facts. But that is the conventional wisdom in Korea today.

Rapid economic development through Japanese financing of Korean firms

Koreans often say that Japan plundered assets from Korea, but that is the complete opposite of the truth. Japan brought in huge sums of investment capital to Korea every year, but until the very end it showed losses, investing more than it took away. These losses were financed by transfer payments from the homeland, borrowing, and issuance of public bonds. Japan kept bringing in more and more money to finance its deficit spending.

Under Japanese rule, Korea achieved average annual GDP growth of about 4 percent, at a time when the average annual growth in many countries was about 2 percent at best. Land was developed through farming, clearing, reclamation, and irrigation. In the early years of annexation, rice production was about 2.3 million cubic yards annually, but this more than doubled to some 5 million cubic yards in 1940.

In the late Joseon Dynasty, living conditions were really harsh. Famine was rampant, and farmers rioted frequently. It was like the extreme poverty in remote regions of North Korea today. Photographs of the central district in front of Seoul's Namdaemun from that time show buildings standing closely side by side, one-story houses with dilapidated thatched roofs. The scene looks like a slum. Isabella Bird, a British explorer-writer, visited Korea during the late Joseon Dynasty (1894-97), and felt ill because of the bad smell in Seoul. She wrote:

"For a great city and a capital, its meanness is indescribable. Etiquette forbids the erection of two-storied houses, consequently an estimated quarter of a million people are living on 'the ground,' chiefly in labyrinthine alleys, many of them not wide enough for two loaded bulls to pass, indeed barely wide enough for one man to pass a loaded bull, and further narrowed by a series of vile holes or green, slimy ditches, which receive the solid and liquid refuse of the houses, their foul and fetid margins being the favorite resort of half-naked children, begrimed with dirt, and of big, mangy, blear-eyed dogs, which wallow in the slime or blink in the sun" (Isabella L. Bird, *Korea and Her Neighbors*, printed originally in 1898 by Fleming H. Revell Co. and reprinted in 2012 by Forgotten Books, p. 40).

This kind of situation changed dramatically once Korea came under Japanese rule. Modern buildings started to appear, and within a short time, Seoul changed and became one of the cleanest, most modern cities in Asia.

The population increased sharply, and the food situation improved significantly. Nutrition improved, health care advanced, infant mortality declined by a wide margin. All this would have been impossible had Japan really been a rapacious colonial overlord. By 1945, when Japanese rule ended, the population was more than double the level of 1905, when Korea became a Japanese protectorate. During the Joseon Dynasty, by contrast, population growth was quite low.

Korea's Population	
Year	Population (in millions)
1753	7.3
1850	7.5
1906	9.8
1910	13.12
1920	16.91
1930	19.68
1940	22.95
1944	25.12

Source: The Government-General in Korea.

During Japanese rule, 80 percent of Koreans lived in rural farming villages. According to data from 1938, 75.7 percent of Koreans engaged in agriculture, 7.5 percent in commerce and transportation, and 2.9 percent in civil services and self-employment. Of course, life changed in urban areas, but it changed even more in rural areas. After suffering chronic and extreme poverty, farmers came to enjoy greater bounty. Farmers, who accounted for the overwhelming majority of the population, benefited more than anyone else from Japanese rule. What would have happened in Korea had it not been ruled by Japan? The answer, even only with respect to living conditions, is as clear as day.

True reasons for changing names and creating family names

People in Korea commonly believe the Japanese colonial administration forced Koreans to adopt Japanese names. That is untrue.

From the outset, the Government-General did not allow the adoption of names that were confusing to people in Japan. The government imposed strict limitations on Koreans registering Japanese-style names when children were born. There were several reasons for this limitation. Toward the end of the Joseon Dynasty, the household registration system was reformed, and many Koreans tried to register Japanese-style names. This created confusion about the restrictions. The Government-General continued to use the policy that prevailed at the end of the Joseon Dynasty. Many Koreans, particularly those who had frequent contact with China, or who lived in Manchuria, wanted to be allowed to use Japanese-style names in addition to Korean-style names. They felt the prohibition of using Japanese-style names was segregation against Koreans.

This view prompted the Government-General to reverse the policy and allow Koreans to use Japanese names. Another reason was that the Government-General came to the conclusion that the assimilation of Korean people would be easier if Koreans used the same surname for husband and wife, as in Japan, Europe, and America, instead of the Korean tradition where the wife retains her maiden name. For these reasons, in 1939 the Government-General allowed Korean people to freely adopt Japanese-style names (1939 Regulation, Number 20).

The new system allowed people to create a new family name, completely different from their Korean family name and given name. The regulations allowed people to change their full name, but it did not compel them to change to a Japanese name.

The system had three stipulations:

(1) Creation of a family name is based on a voluntary reporting system within a six-month period. Those not reporting within this period had to continue using their existing Korean-style family-lineage name as their family name.

(2) The creation and recording of a new family name did not cause the existing family lineage to disappear. The original family-lineage name, together with the given name, remained in the household registration.

(3) Given names could be changed at any time.

As these three stipulations make clear, the system was voluntary, not mandatory. Ultimately, 80.34 percent of the population exercised the option to create a family name, but only a small number of people changed their given name. The policy allowed people to keep their given names even if they created new family names, and many did so as a way to express individual character.

Japanese education expanded use of Hangul and Chinese characters

The Government-General put in place the same normal school system as in Japan and provided education on Japanese language, Korean language, mathematics, Japanese history, Korean history, and traditional Korean ethics, mainly at public schools. It promoted the establishment of a national university (Gyoungsung National University, a predecessor of Seoul National University), and the development of literature and art. About 1,000 new schools were opened, of various types.

At the time of annexation, there were only about 100 normal schools (four-year primary schools), but this number increased steadily. In 1943, there were 5,960 People's Schools (six-year primary schools).

The Government-General provided education in Hangul, Chinese characters, and Japanese language. Korea's literacy rate improved significantly. In 1910, the year of annexation, literacy in Korea was estimated at only about 6 percent. No official surveys on literacy existed until 1930, when the Government-General conducted a national census survey. According to this survey, literacy in Hangul for all age groups was around 22 percent. However, I think this figure is highly inaccurate.

The agriculture survey of 1931, covering 7,366 individuals and 1,249 households in 133 villages in 43 counties, included some information about literacy. According to a report analyzing this survey, 57.0 percent of males and 22.4 percent of females could read Hangul; 51.5 percent of males and 16.4 percent of females could write Hangul. More than 30 percent of males could read and write Chinese, and about 20 percent of males could read and write Japanese (Lee Hung-gu, [Rural Economy in Korea] [Hansung]). These figures suggest a higher rate of literacy than the 1930 census. Another survey conducted in 1944, near the end of the annexation period, shows literacy higher than 60 percent. I believe this figure is a more accurate reflection of reality.

South and North Korea both use the Hangul script that Saejong the Great, fourth king of Joseon, invented in 1443. Hangul is a purely phonetic script depicting the sounds of the Korean language and is completely different from Chinese characters.

Hangul was invented in Korea, with no thought given to the writing of Chinese. Japan had taken quite a different route several centuries earlier, using Chinese characters, but assigning them new pronunciations from the Japanese language. Koreans used Chinese characters for Chinese, and Hangul for Korean. They were completely independent of one another. Hangul also has no relationship to the several different scripts used in Japan.

Some government officials and intellectuals who regarded Chinese characters with reverence were disdainful of Hangul and rejected its use. As a result, Hangul was seldom used for over 400 years. It was only toward the end of the Joseon Dynasty that Korean people finally started to use Hangul in poems and novels. It was through the school system during Japanese rule that people started to use Hangul widely.

Basically, what was needed in Korea was a way of writing Korean that combined Chinese characters and Hangul, the way Japan mixed Chinese characters and kana. This way of writing Korean began to be used by a small segment of the population toward the end of the Joseon Dynasty. However, it did not come into general use until 1886, when the newspaper *Hangjong Weekly*, in the role of official gazette, used Hangul printing type manufactured in Japan, based on an invention by Fukuzawa Yukichi.

In the school system established and promoted by Japanese, the use of Hangul and Chinese characters became widespread.

Shift toward more aggressive assimilation

A Korean *Middle School History Textbook* first printed in 1997 and approved by the national government included this passage. "After the second half of the 1930s, Imperial Japan, in order to carry out the invasion, looted our belongings and human resources, while implementing the policy of erasing our people and our culture." The textbook noted the "Plan for Imperial Japan to Erase the (Korean) People," and said Imperial Japan:

(1) attempted to make Koreans become Japanese, to erase the Korean people in the name of unifying Korea with Japan, making Koreans imperial subjects.

(2) prohibited the use of the Korean language and mandated the use of Japanese language.

(3) prohibited the teaching of Korean history.

(4) forced Koreans to use Japanese names.

(5) built Shinto shrines in various places and made Koreans worship there.

(6) made children memorize the oath of Imperial Japan's subjects.

This list is all the textbook has to say about the "Plan for Imperial Japan to Erase the People." No real content of the plan is given. The same is true of the *High School History Textbook*.

Korea continues to maintain that Koreans were forced to become subjects of Imperial Japan, that they were made to worship Japanese gods, were prohibited from using their own language, lost their culture, lost their traditions, were trampled down, were treated like slaves, humiliated, etc. But Korea does not teach any specific information about any of these accusations. I came to know the truth only after I came to Japan.

When the Second Sino-Japanese war broke out in 1937, the "Oath of Imperial Japanese Subjects" was issued in Korea, and students began reciting it at school every morning. Plans were made to build Shinto shrines in every village, and recommendations were made for visiting the shrine and paying respects there. In 1938, Korean language classes were eliminated, and Korean students started to use the same textbooks as Japanese students.

These developments were followed by new policies for creating family names and changing given names, the abolition of Korean-language newspapers, the military draft system (April 1944) replacing the voluntary system in place at that time, and the draft system for workers (September 1944) replacing the system of solicitation and voluntary arrangements for employment in place at that time. Such aggressive assimilation policies were pushed hard during these years. In Japan this was called the "policy for unification of the Japanese homeland and Korea" or the "policy for making the Korean people Imperial Japanese subjects." In Korea it was called the "plan for Imperial Japan to erase the (Korean) people."

These policies represented a response to impending war, to aggressively assimilate the Korean people into the Japanese people, with a view to establishing a "national unity regime." These events did not take place until the last seven years of Japanese rule in Korea. What changed?

Most Koreans cooperated with Japan during the war

The Government-General pushed policies aimed at Korean assimilation and unification in the areas of governance, economy, society, and culture. It did not aim to maintain a relationship of controller/controlled between the different races, as the Western powers did. Japan took the time to formulate appropriate priorities and implement its assimilation policy.

As already discussed regarding electoral system reform, the Government-General formulated and implemented a long-term plan for compulsory education as well. At that time, Korea did not have a system of compulsory education like Japan's. From a budgetary standpoint, it was difficult to accommodate all the students who wanted to go to school. At the end of Japan's rule, primary school enrollment in Korea was about 60 percent for boys and 40 percent for girls.

The Government-General made plans to implement the same compulsory education system as in Japan starting in fiscal 1946. As a test case, the system was introduced in Pyeong-ham Nam-do with a special budget, and all the children who wanted to enter school were admitted.

The war was a major obstacle in executing the original plan for gradual assimilation. To carry out the war under the national unity policy, the Government-General shifted to a more aggressive assimilation policy. While this was very unfortunate, this was a mere fraction of the period of Japanese rule in Korea.

Just before the war ended, Korean-language education was

terminated. The Government-General did not prohibit the use of the Korean language in everyday life, but its actions were misunderstood, and people believed there was a ban on the Korean language. Most Korean-language newspapers were abolished in 1940, but the Government-General continued to publish the *Meilsinbo* and official bulletins in the Korean language. Both of these measures were taken to solidify efforts for national unity. England prohibited the use of the Irish language during wartime for similar reasons, but Japan did not prohibit the use of the Korean language.

Visits to Shinto shrines and paying respects there were not necessarily forced upon Koreans, either. When primary schoolchildren accompanied by a teacher were to visit a Shinto shrine, a Korean student said to the teacher, "My parents have been telling me that, since I am a Christian, I should not visit the Shinto shrine." The teacher said to this student, "Well, then, wait here," and the teacher left the student outside the shrine. This is a story I myself heard directly from the person who was that student.

Korea's Confucian tradition of respect for ancestors, called "Jae-rae," was not discouraged; it was encouraged. Japan respectfully protected and cherished traditional Korean culture.

Koreans insist on emphasizing measures they say Japan forced upon Korea. However, there were no riots, rebellions, or strong resistance movements in Korea or in Japan against these "aggressive assimilation policies," even during the war. The great majority of Korean people showed no great resistance, and by and large cooperated with Japan in an orderly manner during the war.

As long as their peaceful normal daily lives were not violated,

Korea's general public chose to abide by the legal system, without fighting the colonial rulers and without waving the flag of the anti-Japan independence movement. Korean people welcomed benevolent government by a foreign nation control, rather than evil domestic government. This is how the common people are.

When wartime systems went into action and crises started to affect their way of life, Koreans cooperated with Japan's wartime policies to protect their own lives, just as Japanese people did.

Had Korean women been forced into sex slavery, riots would have resulted

In Korea under Japanese rule, Japanese and Koreans lived in friendship with one another. Based on my own interviews with Korean people who experienced life under Japanese rule (*People's Lives During the Japanese Period of Rule*), I know that Japanese and Koreans, recognizing the good in each other, interacted without major problems in their neighborhoods, workplaces, and schools though there were minor frictions and conflicts.

The issue of comfort women is very important in this regard. Of course, there were comfort women during the war. But military personnel and military police never forced Korean women to become comfort women. It would not have been possible for Japanese and Koreans to live together in friendship if that sort of thing had happened openly.

One Japanese who used to work in the Government-General of Korea said it was not possible for police to force Korean women to go to comfort stations. No such report of coercion was ever delivered to the Government-General. Korean people would not have sat silent about it if it had happened. He said there would undoubtedly have been riots if Korean women had been forced to work as comfort women. A Japanese who attended Su-won Elementary School in Kyouki-do and Kyoungsung Middle School in Seoul said:

"Suppose someone said I abducted a girl in a village. I would have been charged with the crime of abduction and been sent to prison. Even before it became a legal matter, I would be beaten up by Korean villagers. I cannot believe Koreans would sit idle after seeing Korean women taken away forcibly, or that Koreans would be such cowards. People's sense of communal bonds is strong in villages, and so is nationalism. There is no reason why they would sit idly by and tolerate such a thing in silence. On many occasions, I have seen their love for their country, their strong sense of nationalism, and even now I remember. In such a world, it is not possible to abduct women." (*People's Lives During the Japanese Period of Rule*)

In my personal interviews with Koreans who lived under Japanese rule, I never encountered anyone who said he/she had witnessed such a scene or even heard such rumors. That is why there were no anti-Japan riots in Korea after the 3.1 Independence Movement.

Gradual assimilation process

Many Koreans talk about their close friendships with Japanese during the period of Japanese rule, but there are also those who do not talk about such relations and instead talk only about facts. One Korean who graduated from Kyoungsung Imperial University said he had never seen Korean women taken away by force but said it must have happened, given the current debate. This person had a variety of complaints about Japanese rule, but said the following about Japan:

"I personally had friendly relationships with Japanese and do not have any animosity toward them. I have personally never witnessed or heard that Japanese instilled fear in Koreans, or that Japanese beat Koreans or did nasty things to Koreans. However, I did not like the policies implemented by the Government-General.

"Creation of family names and changing given names was supposed to be voluntary under the law, but there were unspoken pressures. My family did not change our name, but most Koreans did. I do not know of any people who were persecuted because they did not change their name. Policemen in charge of villages visited each region and recommended the change of names.

"As for visiting and paying respects at Shinto shrines, all students were taken to visit the shrines. But those who didn't visit were not severely criticized" (op. cit.).

I think these tales are typical of the way the majority of Korean people lived their lives. Accordingly, I believe that if there had been no war, and if the early period of annexation had carried on, assimilation under Japanese rule would have progressed gradually, while maintaining Korea's traditions and national culture.

What if Korea had been ruled by Russia?

In Korea, there is a theme that is considered taboo: What would have happened to Korea if a country other than Japan had colonized it? There is a scholar in Korea who was socially castigated for touching on this theme: Han Seung-jo, professor emeritus at Koryo University. He published an article in a Japanese magazine, "Foolish Crime of Convicting the Pro-Japan Influences Based on Communism and Left-Wing Thoughts: Re-evaluation of the Japan-Korea Annexation" (*Seiron*, April 2005). The article created a big controversy.

In the article, Han described Japan's colonial control over Korea as a blessing, because Korea was not annexed to Russia instead. As a result of the publication of this article, Han was vilified all over the country and ostracized. In the end, he lost all his honor and status.

Between the Sino-Japanese War and the Russo-Japanese War, there was a strong possibility that Russia could have annexed Korea. Japan won its war against the Qing Dynasty, but Japan bent to the pressures of the "Triple Interference" from Russia, Germany, and France. After that, the Joseon Dynasty abandoned its overtures to Japan and started to maneuver to get Russia's protection. At that time, Korea had a pro-Japan government and was undertaking domestic reforms aimed at modernization.

Korea's King Gojong feared Japan's increasing influence. Together with a pro-Russia politician and a Russian diplomat, he fled to the Russian legation, guarded by Russian officers. He unilaterally proclaimed the sovereignty of the king and ousted the pro-Japan government. As soon as he left the Russian legation, he declared that Korea would be known as Imperial Korea. Without a doubt, if Japan had avoided confrontation with Russia and had not triggered the Russo-Japanese War, Korea would have been annexed to Russia. Han was purged from society merely for pointing this out.

At that time, Russia was an absolute monarchy and a superior military power. If Russia had colonized Korea, it would undoubtedly have governed by oppression. When the Russian Revolution erupted in 1917, Korea would have been turned into a communist country, and there is no doubt the entire Korean Peninsula would have been like North Korea.

Chapter VI

Dead End for South Korean Society

Deepening social polarization

Yi Kwang-su, the "Father of Modern Korean Literature," said in 1922 that people should break away from the independence movement that instigated armed fights and terrorist activities. "Independence will not be achieved by the independence movement. It will be achieved only if the people develop the real power to be worthy of independence" ("Argument for Reforming the People," *Kaebyok*, May 1922).

Yi Kwang-su listed five points needing reform, one of which was "anti-social selfishness." Others included "lack of interest in public affairs and the common good, extreme selfishness regarding themselves, their own families and groups." As mentioned in chapter II, Park Chung-hee argued that the "Selfish Party Doctrine" is the "Korean race's challenge for reforming the people." Antisocial selfishness is a doctrine of collective selfishness and has spread throughout Korea's spheres of politics, economy, and society. It is spreading even now, and it could lead to a serious crisis and social collapse.

South Korea faced a risk of national bankruptcy in the currency crisis of November 1997. The economy came under the management of the International Monetary Fund, and the Kim Tae-jung government implemented strong reforms that should greatly enhance the efficiency of market mechanisms. Kim's successor, Roh Moo-hyun, carried on these reform policies and added even more rigorous reforms.

In the 10 years from 2002 to 2011, the economy managed to recover. Economic growth averaged a healthy 4 percent annually, except in 2008 and 2009 when global financial markets were rocked by the collapse of Lehman Brothers.

As South Korea recorded healthy growth and trade surpluses, large corporations such as Samsung Electronics Co. enjoyed rising profits. Many people in Japan noted South Korea's economic success, and some Japanese businessmen said they needed to learn some lessons from South Korea. In contrast, I noted the significant worsening of living standards and structural problems in South Korea and argued constantly that South Korea's economy had failed.

Why the South Korean economy had failed was clear. Workers' wages and salaries had increased, but profit margins at both conglomerates and small enterprises widened more, causing growing income inequality between rich and poor. Only the wealthy, the big conglomerates, and large companies were enjoying true prosperity.

While most people lauded South Korea for having accomplished solid economic growth in the period 2002–11, in reality this had created an increasingly polarized society.

Income inequality

Workers' Income

The top quintile's share of total income continued to increase, reaching 41.6 percent in 2009. The bottom quintile's share was only 8 percent. Low-wage earners accounted for 25.6 percent of the workforce, highest among OECD (Organization for Economic Cooperation and Development) countries.

Income taxes paid by the top quintile of South Korea's earners in 2010 accounted for 84.2 percent of the total; the top 10 percent of earners accounted for 68 percent. (*Chosun Ilbo*, September 17, 2011)

According to the South Korea Tax Research Institute's analysis of data from 2006, the top 1 percent of South Korea's earners accounted for 16.6 percent of total income. Among OECD countries, South Korea's figure was second only to the United States' 17.1 percent. Japan's figure was 9.2 percent.

In 2010, labor income as a share of value-added (the portion of total value-added by corporations that is distributed to production workers) fell below 60 percent in South Korea for the first time ever. (In Japan, it has hovered around 70 percent.)

Tax filers' total income (self-employment income)

In the 10 years to 2010, per capita income in the top quintile increased by 55 percent, but in the bottom quintile it declined by 54 percent. The top quintile's income accounted for 71.4 percent of total income, equivalent to 45 times the bottom quintile's income. Self-employment in South Korea, as a share of the total workforce, was the highest among OECD countries; about 6 million to 7 million people were working in small businesses, or around 90 percent.

High unemployment worsening labor market

Unemployment in South Korea in 2010 was officially 3.6 percent, the highest rate since 2003. Based on the International Labor Organization (ILO) standard used in Western nations and Japan, however, South Korea's unemployment rate was estimated to be at least 13 percent. Some estimates are as high as 20 percent. The government estimates the number of the effectively unemployed at about 3,897,000 in 2009, 4,001,000 in 2010, and 3,946,000 in 2011 (South Korea Statistics Bureau's Research on the Population Engaging in Economic Activities, January 2013). In Japan, the number of the effectively unemployed was 2,510,000 in July 2013.

South Korean workers who left their jobs as a result of being fired, not voluntarily, number about 1.13 million a year. Of these, only about 43 percent are able to find a job within one year. Their income from the social safety net system, including unemployment benefits and unemployment insurance, is only 32 percent of what they earned when they were employed. This ratio was the lowest among OECD countries. Furthermore, about 70 percent of the workers who were fired were not eligible to receive unemployment benefits. "Back to Work: Re-Employment, Earnings, and Skill-Use After Job Displacement," OECD, May 2013)

Of South Korean enterprises that employ more than 300

workers, 37.6 percent set the mandatory retirement age at 55 years old, and 23.3 percent at 60 years or older in 2012. In reality, however, it is traditional for South Korean companies to ask workers to retire at age 45.

In 2005, the nonregular employment accounted for 56.1 percent of all employment, and the average wage of nonregular workers fell to just 50.9 percent of regular workers. This has remained little changed even today.

In Japan, the young suffer relatively high unemployment, and the unemployment rate for the young workers (15–24 years old) stood at 8.2 percent in 2011, compared with the overall rate of 4.6 percent. In contrast, in South Korea, unemployment among the young (15–29 years old) was officially 7.6 percent and worsened to 8.3 percent in 2013. According to the Korea Employment Information Center, however, the youth unemployment rate was 16.7 percent. (*Chosun-Ilbo*, November 23, 2011)

The rate of employment for university graduates in Japan in 2012 was 93.6 percent, but in South Korea the same year it was only 59.5 percent. Almost 60 percent of those who found jobs were nonregular workers, with wages and salaries only about half that paid to regular workers.

Increase in poverty, meager social spending

Rapid increase in the number of poor households

The relative poverty rate in South Korea increased to 15.2 percent in 2009, roughly the same as in Japan. Needless to say, the median after-tax income per household used to define poverty is substantially lower in South Korea than in Japan. The number of poor households, defined as households with below-median income, increased by 135,000 from 2,923,000 in 2008 to 3,058,000 in 2009 (18 percent of all households). This is about twice the level of 2007–08. The number of people living in poor households was about 7 million. The absolute poverty rate increased to 11.1 percent in 2009.

It is likely that both the relative and absolute poverty rates are higher than these figures suggest, because they do not include residents of farming and fishing villages, which tend to be poorer than average.

Poverty among the elderly was very high at 45 percent, and since 2010 it has been the highest among OECD members. No other country had a figure higher than 40 percent. The average disposable income of the elderly between 66 and 75 years old was 62 percent of the national average. Again, this figure was the lowest among OECD members. The suicide rate among the elderly in South Korea was twice as high as in Japan.

The pension system in South Korea was established in 1988. Of people at least 65 years old, 72 percent do not receive pensions. Even if they receive pensions, the average monthly pension income is less than 300,000 won per person (about $276 at the September 2013 rate of KW1,087/$).

Basic Living Allowance

The number of South Koreans receiving basic living allowances was 1,576,000 (about 1.76 times the rate in Japan, as a percentage of the population) in 2010. Although the rate of absolute poverty was 11.1 percent, only about 3.1 percent of people received basic living allowances. About 2.4 million people were living on incomes below the minimum living expense, of whom 1.03 million people were unable to receive basic living allowances.

Welfare Spending

Public welfare spending in South Korea has been increasing little by little. As a percentage of GDP, however, this was 9.4 percent in 2009, the second lowest among OECD members, after Mexico (OECD official figures published in 2012). Medical spending, at 8.7 percent of GDP in 2001, was the lowest among OECD countries. Since then, it has declined steadily to 7.5 percent in 2007 and to 6.9 percent in 2010.

Significant increase in household debt

The Japanese-language version of Britain's *Financial Times* warned against the worsening of South Korea's household debt.

"Many advanced countries' consumer debt declined during the past four years, but South Korea's household debt steadily increased. In 2011, it reached 164 percent of disposable income. This is far more than the figure in the United States at the time of the subprime loan crisis.

"South Korea has been suffering stagnation in the export market. It has been trying to rein in the increase in consumer debt without weakening the economy any further, but it is facing a great challenge.

"The use of credit cards has declined, but loans outstanding have increased. As a result, the quality of the debt has deteriorated."

Eric Ruth, an Asian regional economist at Royal Bank of Scotland, pointed out that [South Korea's] government has not been able to deal with the consumer debt problem. He warned that the household sector's debt is about to reach a level that cannot be sustained (*Financial Times* Japanese-language edition, August 22, 2012).

As a percentage of disposable income, household debt increased to 152.9 percent in 2009, 155 percent in 2010, and 164 percent in 2011. Even in the United States during the subprime-loan crisis, household debt declined from 140 percent of disposable income in 2009 to 114 percent in 2012. In Japan, it was in the range of 100–110 percent and relatively healthy.

The total of South Korea's household sector debt was 963.8 trillion won in December 2012, and increased to 980 trillion won in June 2013 (Bank of Korea, August 22, 2013). It was projected to exceed 1,000 trillion won (about U.S.$915 billion at the September 2013 rate of KW1,093/$) by the end of 2013. Total debt of households and self-employment businesses amounted to 1,100 trillion won (about $1 trillion) in June 2012 (*Jungang Ilbo*, August 24, 2012).

Possibility of a South Korean subprime-loan crisis

South Korea's household debt started to increase after 1997, when the currency crisis erupted. As South Korea implemented sweeping structural reforms and improved its financial structure, enterprises stopped borrowing, and demand for bank loans sharply declined. Banks and other financial institutions aggressively encouraged households to use credit cards and began to extend loans to them. The household sector's debt continued to increase at an average of 25 percent per year. Credit card use in South Korea increased to a level eight times Japan's. Large numbers of bankruptcies were seen in 2003, and a kind of depression set in. This was referred to as the "Great Card Uprising in South Korea."

The Great Card Uprising led to a temporary halt in the growth of household debt, but from 2005 the real estate market began to overheat, and mortgage loans increased sharply. In 2011, the rise in housing prices began to stagnate, and in 2012 prices started to fall.

"In June (2012), housing prices in Seoul, Kyounki-do and Inchun City declined by 3–5 percent from a year before, and the pace of decline gradually accelerated." If prices were to decline 25 percent in five years, the house poor would have been damaged even more than during the currency crisis period. Such was an analysis by the Bank of Korea. "Even a 7 percent decline in the price of real estate would cause the amount of new non-performing loans to reach 4 trillion won [about $3.5 billion at the August 2012 exchange rate of KW1,130/$]. This is a huge amount, equivalent to half the net profits recorded by the banking sector last year" (*Chosun Ilbo*, August 3, 2012). In South Korea, a situation was emerging that was comparable to the United States subprime-loan crisis.

Why large external surpluses do not enrich the domestic economy

South Korea has been recording large trade surpluses, which should have contributed to healthy economic growth over the years, but the number of poor people has been increasing. The main reasons for this are: (i) structural inequality in distribution of wealth, and (ii) even though exports have risen to nearly 60 percent of GDP (57.3 percent in January–September 2012), the benefits are not adequately distributed in the domestic economy.

The IT industry, represented by companies like Samsung and LG, and the automobile industry, led by companies such as Hyundai, continue to increase profits.

Large corporations continue to invest abroad because they think the South Korean market—one fifth the size of the Japanese market—is too small for investment.

South Korea's exports have not enriched the country for five main reasons.

(1) Most profits of large corporations are channeled to foreign investment and domestic retained income, removed from domestic circulation.

(2) The level of domestic technology owned by South Korean companies in manufacturing key parts and materials is low by international standards, and these companies' payments of patent royalties increase as their exports increase.

(3) South Korea's exports are mainly inexpensive products, so profit margins are small. Where they compete with Chinese products, South Korean exporters cannot increase the

prices of their exports, and thus the rate of profit is very low.

(4) Large South Korean corporations are carrying huge loads of debt. The total amount of their foreign loans is equivalent to South Korea's GDP, so no matter how much they earn through trade, they have to pay interest abroad, removing cash from the domestic economy.

(5) The share of foreign capital invested in each of the conglomerates exceeds 50 percent, and the share of foreign capital in commercial banks is as high as 75–100 percent. Many companies pay a large portion of their dividends to foreign investors, so little profit remains in South Korea.

Huge income and assets of managers at large corporations

South Korea's large corporations have performed well thanks to export growth, but the living standards of ordinary people have not improved. The gap in society is widening, and the inequality of income distribution is growing worse, in part because executives of South Korea's large corporations are paid huge sums of money.

According to 2010 financial reports submitted to the Financial Supervisory Bureau, the average annual income of executive officers of 100 large corporations was 1.67 billion won ($1.4 million at the average 2010 exchange rate of KW1,134.8/$). This total represents the sum of salaries, capital gains from the sale of stocks, and dividends. As reported by the South Korean newspaper *Chosun Ilbo* (August 3, 2011), four of the top five earners worked for Samsung Group.

1st Place: Lee Yoon-woo, Vice Chairman, Samsung Electronics Co.

41.95 billion won ($37.0 million)

2nd Place: Cheoi Ji-seong, Vice Chairman, Samsung Electronics Co.

18.01 billion won ($15.9 million)

3rd Place: Yun Ju-hwa, President, Samsung Electronics Co.

7.1 billion won ($6.3 million)

4th Place: Cheong Yeon-ju, President, Samsung Distribution Co.

3.44 billion won ($3.0 million)

5th Place: Kim Jin-su, Former President, Cheil Jedang (First Sugar) Co.

3.39 billion won ($3.0 million)

According to *Hangyoreh* (August 2013), the average annual salary of executive directors at Samsung Electronics Co. in 2012 was about 5.2 billion won ($4.6 million).

I do not know how corporate executive compensation in South Korea compares with other countries. There is no doubt, however, that the top 1 percent of income earners accounted for 16.6 percent of total income in South Korea.

In 2012, there were 28 people in South Korea whose wealth exceeded 1 trillion won (about $880 million). The top five were all chairmen or vice chairmen of huge conglomerates (*Union News*, July 1, 2013).

1st place: Lee Geon-hee, Chairman, Samsung Electronics Co.

12.834 trillion won (about $11.3 billion)

2nd place: Cheong Mong-gu, Chairman, Hyundai-Kia Automobile Group

6.822 trillion won (about $6.0 billion)

3rd place: Lee Jea-yong, Vice Chairman, Samsung Electronics Co.

3.865 trillion won (about $3.4 billion)

4th place: Cheong Le-sun, Vice Chairman, Hyundai Automobile Co.

3.484 trillion won (about $3.1 billion)

5th place: Shin Dong-bin, Chairman, Lotte Group

2.397 trillion won (about $2.1 billion)

Lee Geon-hee, his wife, and each of their four children held assets of more than 1 trillion won, and the total was 20.779 trillion won (about $18.3 billion).

Extremely unhealthy income and profit structure of large conglomerates

Samsung's sales outside South Korea are 85 percent of its total sales. Of this amount, 45 percent are goods produced in South Korea and sold abroad, while 55 percent are both produced and sold abroad. The structure of sales is about the same for LG.

South Korean conglomerates all set higher prices in the domestic market than in overseas markets for the same products.

For example, Samsung's Galaxy S3 smart phone has a price tag of 994,400 won in South Korea, but a significantly lower price equivalent to 736,650 won in the United States (May 2012). Products such as powdered milk, cosmetics, and vitamins all had higher prices in South Korea.

These conglomerates are pursuing strategies to set lower prices abroad to increase market share. They set higher prices in the domestic market to increase their profit margins. Profits are channeled to investment in equipment abroad, in pursuit of further expansion. This is the structure of the flow of funds.

South Korean conglomerates are able to set higher prices in the domestic market because they have oligapolies. In the absence of competition, they set prices as they wish, in contrast to Japan, where competition is stiff. Consumers in South Korea have no choice but to pay the prices that the producers set.

In the Japanese market for mobile telephones, at least six producers compete against each other, including Sharp, Sony, Soft-Bank, and Docomo. In South Korea, however, two companies, Samsung and LG, hold virtually the entire market. In the automobile market, the Hyundai Group—which now holds a 33 percent stake in Kia—commands more than 70 percent of the South Korean market. They sell at higher prices and exploit consumers in the domestic market, and channel their profits abroad to invest and expand their business. There, they sell their products at lower prices, increase market share, and eliminate competitors. This is the basic strategy common to South Korea's conglomerates, and it represents an unhealthy and distorted way of making profits.

Trilemma for large conglomerates

The Samsung Group's sales in 2011 totaled 270.8 trillion won (about $235 billion), or 21.9 percent of South Korea's GDP of 1,235.16 trillion won (about $1,072 billion). This figure was almost equivalent to the government budget of 287.4 trillion won (about $249 billion) (U.S. dollar figures were calculated at the rate of KW1,152/$). Japan's largest company, Toyota, accounted for only 4 percent of Japan's GDP. Total sales of South Korea's 10 conglomerates (Samsung, Hyundai, Kia, SK, LG, GS, Hyundai Heavy Industries, Lotte, Alpha, Hanjin, Dusan) added up to an astonishing 76.5 percent of GDP (according to Conglomerate.com in August 2012). At current stock prices (as of August 24, 2012), 30 conglomerates businesses made up about 60 percent of total market capitalization for all listed companies in South Korea.

Reflecting the national government policy, South Korea's economy is extremely oligopolistic, and sales by the 10 largest conglomerates in 2011 were more than triple the value in 2002. Through 2012, strong growth was seen in current profits, asset values, capitalization, the number of Keiretsu businesses, and the number of employees.

Starting in late 2012, however, things started to head downhill for all conglomerates except Samsung, due to the rapid appreciation of the won. They could not make the profits due to the rapid appreciation of the won.

Dependency on imports for essential parts

South Korean companies depend on imports for essential

parts. Even if these parts can be manufactured in South Korea, patent fees have to be paid abroad. In LCD TV sets, for example, Japanese manufacturers account for 70–75 percent of the world market for polarizing plates and color filters. Japanese and U.S. manufacturers produce 95 percent of glass plates. Japan and Germany make 80 percent of crystal panels. In nonmemory semiconductors, essential parts made in South Korea had no share in four out of eight categories. As a result, Samsung Electronics and LG had to pay huge license fee sums.

Needless to say, Japan has been recording surpluses in technology trade thanks to the strength of the fundamental technologies that Japan has accumulated over the years, but South Korea has been recording large deficits in the technology trade. The "technology trade ratio" is defined as the ratio of technology exports to technology imports. A high ratio reflects a high degree of competitiveness of a country's level of technology. In 2010, the ratio for South Korea was 0.33, meaning the value of South Korea's technology exports was only one-third the value of its technology imports. South Korea was lowest among the 25 OECD countries that provided data on this matter. Japan had a value of 4.6, well ahead of second-place Norway with 2.07. The United States was in sixth place with 1.46.

South Korean enterprises, with their weak manufacturing technology and lack of technological creativity, were, needless to say, vulnerable to being overtaken by latecomers. China became the world's leading manufacturer for 21 items for which South Korea used to hold the same position.

South Korea is now being challenged by China and India

for the lead role in products that need only low or middle-rank technology for manufacturing. For products that require sophisticated technology, South Korea cannot catch up with Japan. As long as South Korea's large enterprises are sandwiched between front-runners and latecomers, they will be cornered, without a future.

Patent royalties

The fees that South Korean enterprises pay for the use of patent licenses are estimated at 10 trillion won ($9.3 billion at the rate of KW1,070.5/$) in 2012. Of course, South Korea earned revenue from its use of these patent licenses, but on balance South Korea recorded large losses.

Debt

In 2011, the debt of Samsung Group as a whole increased 23.9 percent to 276.2 trillion won ($239.8 billion at KW1,152/$), equivalent to the national government budget of South Korea. This amount was greater than Samsung's annual sales. The interest payments were overwhelming.

Other conglomerates also had debt roughly equal to their annual sales. Liabilities of the 30 largest conglomerates totaled 994.2 trillion won at the end of 2011, equivalent to 80 percent of South Korea's nominal GDP of 1,235.16 trillion won in that year.

Corruption of Samsung management

South Korean enterprises have become frequent infringers of other companies' patents. On a list of payers of corporate patent infringement fines in the United States since 1999, four of the top 10 companies were South Korean (*Current Ranking of International Cartels' Payments of Fines in the World, 2010*). Litigation against Samsung, in particular, has been increasing every year. Some places have banned the sale of certain Samsung products.

In August 2012, the U.S. Federal District Court ruled that Samsung had infringed on Apple's patents, and Samsung had to pay $1.05 billion in compensation to Apple. Apple then sued Samsung for an additional $770 million in damages and stopped using Samsung components. Samsung faced other patent litigation as well, and the sum of all the payments was too much for Samsung to pay.

Lawsuits against Samsung were not just about patent infringement. Here are two more cases:

In August 2013, the government of Brazil sued Samsung Electronics for violating labor law, seeking payment of about $108 million. Samsung's factory in Manaus, Brazil, is its largest overseas factory, with about 6,000 workers. These workers sometimes work as much as 15 hours a day, standing 10 hours at a stretch. Some of them have been known to work 27 consecutive days under such cruel conditions. Even before the government suit, the Manaus factory was battling 1,200 legal disputes brought by employees.

Another example: A group of South Korean citizens has accused seven current and former executives of Samsung Distribution Co. of insider trading, and Seoul Central District Court started a breach of trust investigation in June 2013. The suit alleges that Samsung Distribution planned a stock market listing for a mining development company in Kazakhstan, and then sold shares of the mining development company at virtually zero cost to a dummy company set up by former executives of Samsung Distribution. The suit alleges this resulted in losses of about 140 billion won for Samsung Distribution.

Shares of the mining development company were listed on the London Stock Exchange in 2005, earning about 1.2 trillion won ($1.6 billion at the Q3 2013 average exchange rate of KW738/$) for the former Samsung Distribution executives.

This amount should have been subject to South Korean income tax, but it was not, because the former executives were classified as non-residents of South Korea for tax purposes. The profit was made abroad, so South Korea's tax authorities could not touch it.

In Samsung's financial reports, net profit is virtually identical on both a consolidated and parent-only basis. That is because Samsung's subsidiaries are able to transfer profits to the parent company. This distorts the distribution of wealth within the group. If Samsung collapses, it will have a domino effect on its subordinate companies, leading to the collapse of these subordinate companies, with the moral hazard of a complex organization "too big to fail."

End of export-oriented economy addicted to weak currency

South Korea has always been weak in home-grown technology. It imports parts, materials, and machine tools from Japan to produce finished goods for export. This structure remains in place even today. While South Korea earns huge amounts of foreign exchange, it has chronic trade deficits with Japan. South Korea cannot overcome its inability to reduce imports of parts and materials on the one hand and its inability to develop its own technology on the other.

South Korea showed trade surpluses of $40 billion in 2010, $31 billion in 2011, and $38 billion in 2012, according to JETRO's 2013 report on trade and investment. In trade with Japan, however, it showed deficits of $36.1 billion in 2010, $28 billion in 2011, and $25.5 billion in 2012.

After the rapid depreciation of the won from the currency crisis of 1997, South Korea became a country with chronic trade surpluses. The most important cause of South Korea's trade surpluses was that its currency remained depressed for years. The government intervened aggressively in the foreign exchange market to keep the Korean won's value low. But it also had a swap arrangement with Japan to keep the won from collapsing entirely.

It was only thanks to Japan's guarantee that the South Korean government was able to sell won day after day without any worry that the won would just keep falling. That period has come to an end, however, and the won has been appreciating against the yen since 2012.

As the won appreciates, export growth will slow, bringing a risk that South Korea will fall into trade deficits. South Korea may have a strong current-account balance, but that is because it is strong in trade in goods. It remains weak in services. If South

Korea starts to show deficits in trade in goods, it will not be able to cover them with services trade surpluses the way Japan does.

This is a list of weaknesses in South Korea's economy:

- Structure of external debt.
- Structure of oligopoly comprising huge conglomerates.
- Distorted structure of income and profits of huge enterprises.
- High degree of dependence on foreign capital. (Foreign investors could take back their funds from South Korea at a moment's notice if performance deteriorates.)
- Extreme dependence on the China market (40 percent of South Korea's exports go to China).
- Huge payments for patent royalties.
- Huge payments for fines and damages for patent infringement.
- Excessive dependence on Japanese parts used in producing South Korea's exports.
- Low level of South Korea's home-grown technology.
- Low ratio of domestic production.
- Second-rate products that are mainly knock-off goods.
- High rates of defective products.
- Weakness in creativity and tendency to be overtaken by late-comers.
- Difficulty in coping with currency appreciation.

Until 2012, the weakness of the South Korean won helped to paper over these shortcomings. In recent years, however, South Korea has had to face won appreciation, turning these structural weaknesses into more intractable problems.

Rapid increase in embezzlement and fraud

South Korean society has changed dramatically since the period from November 1997 to August 2001 when South Korea received financial support from the IMF, with its economy under IMF management. At that time, South Korea's economy entered a crisis due to failed currency policy and a weak financial system. Under IMF management, South Korea underwent economic reforms and became as open as European nations and the United States—or perhaps even more open. Reform was not gradual, as it was in Japan. The economic order changed drastically in the short span of a few years, causing cracks to form in the social hierarchy.

One series of events symbolize this drastic change. Amid large-scale restructuring, companies instituted labor practices based on evaluations that were extremely competitive and results-oriented. With the survival of many large enterprises hanging in the balance, these new labor practices had a tremendous impact on society.

Around that time, I spoke with my older sister on the telephone. In a rough voice, she told me, "People who were friendly and collegial until just recently are suddenly enemies, stabbing each other in the back to survive. People are even stealing money from their relatives. Things like that are happening every day. Money, money, money is the only thing anyone ever talks about anymore."

South Korea was beset with a violent storm of egoism and mistrust. On the one hand, the ranks of millionaires and even billionaires were growing, but so were the ranks of the homeless, and poor families who could no longer pay for their kids' school lunches or their utility bills. A "survival of the fittest" mentality took hold. In January 2002, a South Korean newspaper said:

"Nowadays, South Korea is in an extreme thrall of money worship, where 'money is everything.' Each passing day brings dozens of new billionaires profiting from unearned income. Many people lost their jobs in the foreign exchange crisis, but money worship is now rampant. In this process, staff members of institutions in charge of various central national functions have been sucked into the maw of corruption. Our spiritual strengths such as courtesy, friendship, respect, filial piety, and loyalty that have long supported us have crumpled. Without revolutionary change, nothing will prevent South Korean society from corruption and downfall." (*Chosun Ilbo*, Japanese-language edition, January 3, 2002)

The "revolutionary change" the newspaper refers to is not expected to take place any time soon. Meanwhile, the rapid spread of corruption is causing South Korea's system of social mores to rattle, on the verge of collapse. Embezzlement and fraud have been endemic in South Korea for a long time, and new instances are becoming more frequent. The table on the next page compares incidents of embezzlement and fraud in South Korea and Japan in 1997 and 2010.

Between these two years, the number of incidences of embezzlement and fraud in South Korea increased by 5,612 and 57,667 cases, respectively. In contrast, in Japan, the number of these incidences of embezzlement increased only slightly, while the number of incidences of fraud decreased. In Japan, the frequent incidences of fraud have been discussed as a serious social problem, but it is clear that the number of the incidences declined between these two years.

In contrast, the number of fraud cases for South Korea was about six times the number for Japan in 2010. However, the reality is much worse for South Korea. The reason is that, in South Korea, if you say that you became a fraud victim, you would be looked down on as a stupid guy, and people say that it is a fault on the part of the cheated. Thus, such cases would not be reported to the police. The fact that South Koreans do not usually report crimes to the authorities is not limited to fraud; indeed, this practice is prevalent in all other cases of crimes except murder.

Incidences of Embezzlement and Fraud in South Korea and Japan

Fiscal Year		1997		2010	
Embezzlement	South Korea	20,171	[43.86]	25,783	[52.10]
	Japan	1,569	[1.24]	1,676	[1.31]
Fraud	South Korea	146,132	[317.74]	203,799	[412.54]
	Japan	49,426	[39.20]	34,602	[27.07]

Figures in brackets indicate the number of incidents per 100,000 people. Data for 1997 are from the UN Office of Drug-Related Crimes. Data for South Korea in 2010 are from South Korea's *2011 Whitepaper on Police*. Data for Japan in 2010 are from Japan's *2012 Whitepaper on Police*.

In South Korea, crimes not reported to the authorities are called "black crimes." The South Korean police's "Report on the Method of Estimating the Number of Black Crimes and the Policy to Minimize the Number" estimates the number of black crimes such as burglary and theft is 18 times the reported number. Even assuming the number of black crimes involving fraud is only 10 times the reported number, the real figure would be an astonishing 2 million.

Steady increase in serious crimes

As the gap between rich and poor widens, social order breaks down, and crime increases in number. Since the 1997 currency crisis, the number of crimes in South Korea has been increasing steadily, and has now reached alarming levels. In recent years, the media in South Korea have been reporting a steady stream of stories on increasing frequency of serious crimes.

"The incidence of serious crime has increased year after year in South Korea for the past 10 years. South Korea's Police Academy conducted research on serious crimes such as murder, burglary, rape, and arson in 2001–2010, and reported that the number of such crimes increased 84.5 percent during that period. The number of rapes increased by 80 percent.

"In a country-by-country analysis of the rate of serious crimes committed per 100,000 residents in 2009 and 2010, conducted by British Police, South Korea ranked 6th in murder and 11th in rape, among the 34 OECD countries." (*Joog Ang Ilbo*, June 1, 2012)

In Japan, the number of serious crimes has been declining over the years, but in South Korea it has been increasing. South Korean society is in a serious crisis.

Reported Number of Serious Crimes in
South Korea and Japan (2011)

Crime	South Korea	Japan
Murder	1,261 [2.55]	1,051 [0.82]
Burglary	4,395 [8.89]	3,673 [2.87]
Arson	3,488 [7,06]	1,087 [0.85]
Rape	19,498 [39.46]	1,185 [0.92]

Figures in [ ] represent the rate of the reported incidences of crimes per 100,000 residents. South Korea's *Highest Investigation Bureau, 2011 Crime Statistics,* and Japan's *National Police Agency, Situation on Crimes in 2011.*

The comparison of crimes committed per 100,000 residents in South Korea and Japan shows that South Korea's rate is 3.1 times Japan's in murder, 3 times Japan's in burglary, 8.3 times Japan's in arson, and 42.8 times in rape. For other crimes, the report shows that South Korea's rate is 9.6 times Japan's in assault (the actual number of cases is about 100,000), 7 times Japan's in inflicting injuries on others (more than 70,000), and 4.1 times Japan's in theft (more than 260,000).

South Korea's legal system is soft on punishing criminals

The rate of reported rape cases in the United States is 30 times that in Japan. The rate in South Korea is about 43 times that in Japan, far exceeding the United States. About 50 percent of sex crimes in South Korea are rapes, and one out of three rapists is a repeat offender. A report by South Korea's Ministry of Gender

Equality and Family entitled "Research on Criminal Violence in the Nation in 2010" said only 6–7 percent of rapes are reported; in reality, it estimated about 200,000 women were victims of rapes in 2010. According to this report, 4 of every 100 women have experienced rape or attempted rape.

South Korea's population is only 38 percent of the population of Japan, but the number of major crimes is greater in South Korea. The number of serious crimes, in particular, is much higher than in Japan. One reason is that the social order is clearly unstable. Another reason is that police, investigators, and courts are too lenient on criminals. About 60 percent of criminals charged with rape receive suspended prison terms or are bailed out. About 30 percent of serious offenders are bailed out.

In Suwon City, capital of Gyeonggi-do with a population of 1 million, only about 28 percent of violent suspects were indicted, and more than 70 percent of them received suspended sentences. In most cases, convicted criminals were fined rather than imprisoned, and the process typically ended with a summary verdict. Only 3 percent of those indicted went to trial (*Chosun Ilbo*, September 17, 2012).

In South Korea, criminals who are intoxicated when they commit crimes receive reduced punishments. Those who commit simple assault (e.g., punching or slapping someone) are likely to be simply fined or to receive a summary indictment. They do not have to go to court, even if they have a criminal record. This is the tradition of the South Korean legal system. For this reason, in South Korea there are criminals with 40 to 50 criminal convictions on their record (op. cit.).

In Japan, it is often said that the "myth of safety is gone," or "Japan has become a dangerous country where crime is rampant." By international standards, however, Japan is still one of the world's safest countries. Its crime rates are among the lowest among OECD countries. Incidence of serious crimes (murder, rape, burglary, arson) is the lowest among OECD members (based on OECD data, UN Office on Drugs and Crime, etc.). Japan's ranking is not the lowest for theft, but items for most thefts in Japan are bicycles. For petty crime, it is clear that Japan has tough surveillance. Also, the number of crimes in Japan has been declining in recent years, according to the official white paper. In Korea, it has been increasing.

Society plagued by hopelessness and corruption of youth

Since 1998, more and more South Korean young people have said they cannot feel proud of their country. The root cause of this disaffection is that young people face serious difficulty in finding jobs. But this lack of pride is not limited to youths who are suffering in "employment hell." The young elite also lack pride in their country.

Koryo University is a first-class university, and many of the students come from wealthy families. This university is nearly as esteemed as Seoul National University. In a survey conducted in 2001 at Koryo University, 51.4 percent of the students responding said, "If I were to be born all over again, I would not wish to be born in South Korea." The same survey was also conducted in other countries, and 75–80 percent of respondents in those countries, including Japan, said they would want to be reborn in their home country. (The survey covered 385 students at universities in seven countries, including South Korea, Japan, France, Russia, and Australia, in commemoration of the 54th anniversary of *Koryo University News*.)

Why would students at a first-class university wish to be born in some other country? They must have no hope in South Korean society. Young people's despair at Korean society seems to start in middle school and may be connected to the fact that South Korean society is plagued by corruption.

Another survey asked students at middle and high schools in Seoul, "Is South Korean society corrupt?" to which 90.5 percent answered yes (survey conducted by "Union of the People Against Corruption," December 10–21, 2001).

Even more surprising is middle and high school students' recognition of corruption. When asked, "If no one is watching you, do you think it is necessary to obey the law?" 41.3 percent of students responded it is not necessary; 33 percent said that if they were to witness misdeeds or corruption, they would ignore it if they thought blowing the whistle might be harmful to themselves. In addition, 28.4 percent said they would commit bribery if they thought it could solve a problem. A great number of young people not only express tolerance for corruption, they even show a willingness to act corruptly.

Spread of injustice

How about since 2002, when the economy started to re-bound? In an October 2005 survey, 78.1 percent of middle and high school students responded that "the South Korean society is corrupt" (survey of 1,000 students nationwide, conducted by the President's "National Cleansing Commission" and "Former Corruption Prevention Commission"). Asked what factors account for this, the top response was that "the world of politics is corrupt," by 48.6 percent of the students. Another 17.9 percent said, "There is no good legal system," and 17.7 percent said, "The social environment is not right." Most students see the problem as lying in the political world, rather than the legal system or the social environment.

Of the 10 presidents of South Korea, two were short-term temporary acting presidents. Of the eight presidents who served full terms, Park Chung-hee was the only one never charged with corruption. Six were investigated for corruption. All had relatives and close associates who were arrested or sentenced to prison. For better or worse, these are the role models in South Korea. "Well known people are doing it, so we can do it, too" is a tradition common not only among children, but among South Korean people in general. It is not easy to root out corruption because, 53.7 percent of people surveyed say, "punishments are too lenient," while 20.7 percent say "it pays," and 19 percent say "obeying the law leads to losses."

In a 2006 survey of middle and high school students, 86.6 percent responded, "Corruption is widespread in South Korea"

("Questions Regarding Recognition of Corruption," covering high school students at seven schools in Daeku, conducted by Korea Transparency Institution Taegu Headquarters). In this survey, no small number of students showed tolerance of corruption and said they themselves might engage in it. For example, 34.7 percent responded affirmatively to the statement: "Even if it meant going to jail for 10 years, I might commit corruption for 1 billion won." Another survey covering people of all ages showed the following results.

"If you were to be born all over again, would you wish to be born South Korean?"

No: 67.8 percent (5,696 people)

Yes: 24.5 percent (2,058 people)

Not sure: 7.8 percent (652 people)

Electronic Bulletin Board, Survey of 8,406 people conducted by "DC Inside," August 23–31, 2006.

In a similar survey in Japan, the results were:

"Do you feel good that you were born in Japan?"

"Good": 94 percent

"Not Good": 3 percent.

Asahi Shimbun, "Survey of National Patriotism" conducted by *Asahi Shimbun*, January 25, 2007.

In this respect, South Korea and Japan are the opposite of one another.

Chapter VII

Can Good Relations Be Restored Between Japan and South Korea?

Abe's foreign policy and the hole in the donut

The government of Japanese Prime Minister Shinzo Abe was actively engaged in diplomatic activities in 2013. Abe telephoned the leaders of the United States, Australia, Indonesia, India, Vietnam, Britain, Russia, and other countries. He dispatched special envoys to South Korea, Myanmar, the Philippines, Singapore, Brunei, Australia, and elsewhere.

Abe himself led the way, personally visiting India, East Asia, Australia, Mongolia, the Middle East, Africa, the United States, Russia, Europe, and Argentina between January and September 2013. Abe visited more countries in such a short period than any other Japanese prime minister.

Japan's mass media called his foreign policy "Global Diplomacy," but *Asahi Shimbun* took a different tack, calling it "Donut Diplomacy." *Asahi Shimbun* was pointing out there was a hole at the center of Abe's diplomacy. For all the countries he had visited, he had not yet visited either China or South Korea, two countries that arguably should have been at or certainly near the top of his list.

China and South Korea were often critical of Abe's foreign policy, calling it a policy of "encircling China." China says, "There is no way Japan can surround China. Japan can only isolate itself." South Korea says, "Japan tried to surround China, but it only isolated itself. Japan is becoming anxious and isolated." Both China and South Korea are using similar language to criticize Japan.

Actually, though, China and South Korea are the ones that have isolated themselves. The hole in the donut is the result of their attitude toward Japan. If they want to fill the hole, they have to do it themselves. The onus is on South Korea and China to show a greater sense of urgency about this issue.

Japanese cooperation with Russia, Taiwan, and Southeast Asia

Japan and Taiwan signed a fishing agreement on April 11, 2013, allowing Taiwan to fish in the area surrounding the Senkaku Islands, which are under joint management by the two governments. The agreement prohibits Taiwanese fishing boats from entering the area within 12 miles of the Senkaku Islands, which Taiwan had been claiming as its own territorial waters. Due to this agreement, China—which also claims sovereignty over the Senkaku Islands—can no longer form a common front with Taiwan against Japan on this issue. Some people in Japan criticized Abe for conceding too much to Taiwan, but he showed excellent and realistic judgment.

On April 28, Abe visited Russia, where he agreed the two

countries should discuss a framework for security cooperation. This arrangement is referred to as the "two-plus-two" forum. Given the history of prickly relations between the two countries, it is quite remarkable that Russia agreed to these discussions.

More recently, Russia has been acting more aggressively regarding national security cooperation between Japan and the United States. Russia has been increasing its national security cooperation not only with Japan and the United States but also with countries in Southeast Asia.

Obviously Russia is concerned about China and the risks of territorial security. Like Japan and the United States, Russia sees China rapidly building up its military and threatening to break out of its national borders.

At the height of tensions between Japan and China over the Senkaku Islands, Russia was unprecedentedly quiet. China proposed to Russia that they form a common front against Japan regarding the Senkaku Islands, but Russia did not respond affirmatively. Russia seems to have strong expectations of Japan in the areas of politics and economic cooperation.

On May 3, 2013, Japan entered into a currency swap agreement with ASEAN countries, but this excluded China and South Korea. More than 50 percent of trade between Japan and ASEAN is denominated in yen. China and ASEAN countries have been enmeshed in a dispute over the Spratly Islands. With the currency swap arrangement, it has become easier for Japanese enterprises to raise local currencies, and this in turn has stimulated investment. The Asian situation surrounding South Korea, China, and Japan is about to change significantly.

South Korea and China have not joined the Trans-Pacific Partnership (TPP). If they remain nonparticipants, the TPP may be established without them. If that happens, China and South Korea will be almost completely isolated. In June China, and in September South Korea suddenly changed their positions and announced they would consider joining the TPP. In the areas of politics and economy, South Korea and China are now standing at the last critical moments of whether they become isolated in Asia.

Danger of the South Korea–China currency swap agreement

In the past, South Korea and Japan had a currency swap agreement. When South Korea grew short of foreign currencies, Japan would guarantee availability and provide foreign currencies to South Korea. This enabled South Korea to maintain the stability of the won, guarding against collapse and securing favorable conditions for exports.

In 2000, Japan, China, and South Korea completed a currency swap agreement with ASEAN countries (Chiang Mai Initiative, or CMI) that was linked with IMF financing. The size of this financial arrangement was $10 billion. In December 2008, the maximum value of withdrawals was increased to $20 billion from $3 billion, as South Korea faced a currency crisis following the collapse of Lehman Brothers. In October 2011, this ceiling was raised further to $70 billion in connection with instability brewing in European financial markets.

Japan announced the possibility of terminating this Japan-Korea currency swap because, on August 10, 2012, President Lee Myong-bak landed on Takeshima (Dok-do). South Korea strongly opposed this announcement by Japan, and twice it did not ask for the extension of the swap arrangement. Instead, South Korea pushed an increase in the size of the swap arrangement with China.

The size of the Japan–South Korea currency swap remained at only $10 billion under the CMI arrangement; the CMI framework is expected to expire in February 2015. South Korea has chosen China as its partner in the swap arrangement.

The size of the current currency swap arrangement between China and South Korea is $58 billion. The two have agreed that the swap arrangement would be used to settle trade transactions between them. In other words, South Korea would break with Japan and depend on China to secure foreign currencies, a drastic change in its monetary and foreign exchange policy, actively cooperating with China in building up its yuan-based economic sphere.

This is precarious, though, because the trade settlement system based on the China–South Korea currency swap arrangement (360 billion yuan) has not been functioning well at all. China's short-term interest rates increased sharply, and the market situation deteriorated. In the first half of 2013, among seven banks in South Korea, only Uri Bank used funds under the China–South Korea swap arrangement, amounting to only 7 million yuan.

The end-date of the China–South Korea currency swap arrangement was extended to October 2017 from October 2014; China was reluctant to accept this change, but South Korea was adamant.

China, armed with its economic power, is in a strong position to exert great influence on South Korea. This possibility is highly dangerous for South Korea.

South Korea trying to return to the days before the Sino-Japanese War

Mr. Takanori Irie, professor emeritus at Meiji University, gave a talk some time ago about East Asia with respect to the Korean Peninsula. He noted quite convincingly that from a geopolitical point of view, the current situation strongly resembles conditions prevailing on the eve of the Sino-Japanese War (*Voice*, "East Asia on the Eve of the Sino-Japanese War," December 2003).

His thoughts reflected the geopolitical situation one year after Roh Moo-hyun came to power. South Korea had started to show a foreign policy that leaned markedly pro–North Korea and anti-Japan, distancing itself from both Japan and the United States, and getting closer to China and Russia.

Irie said that before the Sino-Japan war, Japan wanted to shield South Korea from the influence of Imperial China. Japan was concerned about possible control of South Korea by the continental powers. Japan had similar concerns on the eve of the Russo-Japanese War. Irie argued that Japan's understanding of national security at that time was that it must, by all means, prevent Russia from controlling the Korean Peninsula.

"The essence of the Sino-Japanese War and the Russo-Japanese War rested in the view above. Japan won these two wars and kept the Korean Peninsula out of the control of the continental powers. Finally Japan, as an oceanic nation, was able to keep geopolitical balance in East Asia," Irie said.

Under Roh Moo-Hyun, South Korea started to act as if it wanted to bring back the days before the Sino-Japanese War.

South Korea started to deepen its relations with North Korea, and North Korea started to rely on China. China exerted influences on North Korea and wanted to take leadership of the Six-Nation Conference on North Korea. North Korea, in turn, made efforts to maintain relations with Russia, while Russia tried to maintain its unique relationship with North Korea.

During Roh Moo-Hyun's presidency of South Korea, the situation in the region seemed to be returning to the situation prevailing before the Sino-Japanese War, as Professor Irie discussed.

Professor Irie said there has been no fundamental change in the geopolitical balance between the "continental nations" (China and Russia), "peninsula nations" (North and South Korea), and the "oceanic nation" (Japan).

"There are many points in common between China under the Qing Dynasty and China under the current one-party communist regime. Both were concerned about management of water and capturing the people's hearts. Both also faced a crisis situation with rampant corruption that might lead to the collapse of the nation. China is expanding its military power to divert the people's attention away from this domestic crisis, and it has been trying to build strong economic power based on traditional sinocentric ideology.

"It must be said that the Russian Empire in the past and Russia of today are essentially the same, a continental nation with a certain structure.... In many ways, Japan may be the only country in East Asia that has changed greatly in the past 100 years."

Professor Irie's argument is 10 years old, but now more than ever, South Korea appears to be trying to put itself under the protection of China. The current situation is coming to closely resemble conditions prevailing before the Sino-Japanese War.

For centuries, the Korean Peninsula was under the dominant influence of Imperial China and survived by subjugating itself to China both politically and culturally. South Korea today might be trying to return to the situation of the past, seeking peace under the strong influence of China.

South Korea, North Korea, and China are the only countries in the world where government and the media have been loudly denouncing the "militaristic, reactionary Abe government." If these countries keep this up, they will end up isolated from the international community.

Korea did not shed its own blood

Japan-Korea relations are now at an all-time low. Is there any way that Japan and South Korea can become friendly? It will be very difficult, but I still think there is a way. South Korea must "cut its own flesh" and "shed its own blood."

Since South Korea was established in the aftermath of World War II; South Korea has seen Japan bleed, but it has never shed its own blood. There have been only two occasions when South Korea came close to "shedding its own blood," but both times, it turned away.

This idea was shared by the leaders of South Korea's military governments, Park Chung-hee, Chun Doo-Hwan, and Roh Tae-woo, who believed that in order for South Korea to become truly independent, it had to become friends with Japan and serenely shed its own blood.

Park Chung-hee said, "Annexation of Korea to Japan was Korea's own choice."

Chun Doo-hwan said, "South Korea must take an attitude of self-reproaching its own responsibility seriously."

Roh Tae-woo said, "South Korea must reflect on itself that it could not defend itself in the past."

These remarks would surely be political suicide for these three leaders if they were made in today's South Korea.

The three former military presidents continued to promote anti-Japan education in South Korea, but they all thought South Korea could not move forward by maintaining the status quo. They all wanted to open an avenue to the construction of a new South Korea based on "self-reproach and self-reflection." These pronouncements by Chun Doo-hwan and Roh Tae-woo, on solemn official occasions, showed they wanted to open such a road. This was the first opportunity for South Korea to "shed its own blood."

The main obstacle, however, was the anti-Japan education that these presidents themselves had continued to promote. This had become a sacred cow that even they could not violate. The presidents' remarks fell on deaf ears.

In 1993, Kim Young-sam became South Korea's first civilian president. He demolished the historic building of the Government-General of Korea, which had been transformed into a museum, because he said it was a "symbol of Imperial Japan." South Korea had become a nation defined by its anti-Japan stance. The government showed no inclination to move toward "self-reproach and self-reflection" and held fast to the anti-Japan posture of its predecessors, which has continued in the civilian government of today.

Self-reproach and self-reflection repressed by anti-Japan influence

South Korea's second opportunity to "shed its own blood" emerged in November 1997, when its economy was on the brink of possible collapse in the aftermath of the currency crisis. South Korea's economy came to a complete standstill and was put under the control of the IMF. South Koreans tasted the bitterness of defeat, and this led some to show signs of moving toward self-reflection. Expressions like "coming to terms with Korea's own past" came to be heard, and books related to this idea appeared. Some people even started to say, "Let's learn from Japan."

Then, however, Kim Tae-jung took office immediately after the currency crisis. He ignored such voices, maintained the anti-

Japan policy of his predecessors, and led the country in the direction of making friends with North Korea.

When Roh Moo-hyun came to power, he continued to seek closer ties with North Korea, but he upped the ante by switching from "coming to terms with Korea's own past" to "erasing the influence of pro-Japan groups." His administration strongly suppressed pro-Japan groups. The government, and the broader society, suppressed ideas related to "self-reproach and self-reflection" and the review of history under Japan rule. This situation continues even today.

Why are South Koreans so reluctant to shed their own blood? There is a tremendous gap between South Korean values and Japanese values. Without understanding this difference, it is impossible for Japanese and South Koreans to simply say, "Let's be friends."

Shi Hei, a critic born in mainland China, says China may be able to eliminate misunderstanding of or prejudice against Japan if the regime in China changes or if the Chinese government changes its anti-Japan policy. In the case of South Korea, however, it may never be possible to change anti-Japan policy even with a change in government. Significant change will only occur if the South Korean people embrace self-reproach and self-reflection. This possibility, however, is remote.

Korea's campaign for new history textbooks

South Korea today is unlikely to revise its pro–North Korea, anti-Japan policy stance, but it is not completely impossible. Some South Korean intellectuals are already engaged in writing new history textbooks, just as some Japanese are. The Japanese press has seldom reported on this development. In the middle of 2013, the following was reported in Japan:

"On June 24, in a room at the Press Center in the heart of Seoul, a group that includes well-known conservative scholars and journalists among its members made a declaration."

The scholars were members of the group "Gathering of Intellectuals Concerned About Distortion of History and Suppression of Freedom of Learning." Their declaration had a tendentious title: "Denounce the Democratic Party—left-wing opposition parties and the former Democratic United Party." More than 400 people, including researchers and journalists, endorsed this declaration.

Members of South Korea's Democratic Party had conducted a special investigation into conservative writers in connection with a high school textbook, *Modern History of Korea*, published by the South Korean publisher Education House. Conservative groups decried the investigation, calling it equivalent to censorship and suppression of the freedom of learning. One supporter of the declaration compared the Democratic Party investigation to Qin Shi Huang, the first emperor of China, who burned books and killed scholars in the second century b.c. (MSN Sankei "News and Beat," July 7, 2013).

The Japanese press report went on to say, "According to sources familiar with the issue, the textbook argues against the traditional view that Japanese rule was characterized by cruel colonial policies and courageous resistance to the ruler, and it includes references to the way in which the vast majority of the Korean people actually carried on their lives, to their efforts and to results in various aspects."

South Korea's government cannot openly suppress scholastic research reexamining the history of Japanese rule as long as it remains within the scope of scholastic study. But when research takes the form of critiques or general magazine articles, this has at times led to the banning of books and magazines. Some writers have been sued for defamation. Such critiques have also been known to prompt newspapers and TV to conduct extensive campaigns criticizing the writers. Bloggers then accuse the writers as traitors and ostracize them. Many people have suffered this kind of treatment.

Critiques that remain behind academic walls do not usually generate any response at all in the broader society. This means the impact of such scholastic work is in fact very limited. Ironically, this is a blessing for academic work. That is reality in South Korea today.

Domestic dispute over understanding history

One South Korean intellectual who has continued research on the reexamination of Japanese rule is Lee Young-hoon, professor emeritus of economics at Seoul National University and a top representative of the group of intellectuals concerned about distortion of history and suppression of freedom of learning.

For many years, Lee has called it a big mistake to argue that the Korean people suffered poverty under Japanese rule because of Imperial Japan's one-sided plundering of property. He argues that significant economic development was accomplished in Korea under Japanese rule, and the transfer of modern capitalism at that time was an important factor contributing to the rapid economic growth since the 1960s (*Korean Daily*, interview, April 22, 2004).

The group of scholars including Professor Lee has conducted joint research for about 20 years, and the results were published as *Understanding Again the History of the Period Before and After Liberation* (two volumes, Book World Pub. Co., February 8, 2006). Their book was framed as a response to an earlier book, *Understanding the History of the Period Before and After Liberation* (first volume published in 1979, followed by five more volumes). The content of the new book was meant to correct earlier book's errors and biases.

On the basis of the 2006 scholarly work, the group also published a new high school textbook, *Modern History of Korea*. No schools have adopted this textbook, but it is sold in bookstores. This was an epoch-making development in Korea.

Modern History of Korea was cleared by the textbook approval process in the previous year. Members of the Democratic Party, however, launched an investigation against the writers, demanding detailed accounts of expenses for field trips, results of research projects, etc. This investigation prompted the conservative scholars and journalists to make the declaration referred to above.

This textbook passed the screening process in September 2008.

From the day of the passage, the publishing company has received harassing telephone calls on a daily basis, faulting the book for "approving of Japanese colonization" and "distorting history," and demanding that publication be halted.

In Japan, the public generally supports the idea of new textbooks for Japanese history. In Korea, though, this is no more than an arena for a clash of intellectuals. The general public takes little interest in the subject.

Many well-known scholars from South Korea, the United States, and other countries participated in writing *Understanding Again the History of the Period Before and After Liberation.* It has not been possible, though, to break down the solid walls of anti-Japan education. This is because anti-Japan education has been at the core of education in South Korea for over 60 years. This education binds South Korean people's understanding of their history to the psychological and political environment of the present day.

Interpersonal relationships in Japan and South Korea

Value systems and emotional attitudes in South Korea are different from those in Japan, and this difference exacerbates the difficulty of maintaining a healthy relationship between the two countries.

There are many ways in which the Japanese perspective seems to be completely opposite from those of South Koreans and Chinese. Generally speaking, if South Koreans and Chinese want to build a relationship with someone, they try to be as friendly as possible right from the beginning. Japanese, by contrast, generally keep their distance from others in the beginning, and they close this distance only gradually. South Koreans often wonder if Japanese people really want to be friends.

South Koreans think true friendship is as close as a kinship relationship. This is the South Korean tradition stemming from the lineage-based society. South Koreans want friends to respond the way family members would, and they try to form close relationships with people as soon as they sense they are on the same wavelength. South Koreans tend to close the distance between themselves and others as soon as possible, and they behave as if they have been friends for a long time.

If their efforts to establish friendship quickly are rejected, they may become hostile.

To put it baldly, South Koreans tend to see human relationships in black-and-white. People are either their friends or their enemies. This mode of thinking can be extended to groups and even nations.

In the past, political leaders in South Korea and China were somewhat different from the current leadership in terms of relations with Japan. For example, in South Korea before the civilian government and in China before Jiang Zemin's regime, leaders on both sides were able to set aside territorial disputes and focus on more substantive issues. In short, South Korea and China used to be able to overlook—at least temporarily—a distance they could not bridge, and keep it from becoming a major sticking point.

That is how leaders in the past maintained their relationship with Japan.

Today's leaders in South Korea and China are not like that. They want to close the distance at a single stroke of a pen. If Japan rejects their way of closing the distance and stands aloof, China and South Korea turn hostile, as Shi Hei has noted. South Korea and China have more of a buddy-buddy style. These two countries of today are repeating a tradition they practiced generations ago.

The shorter the distance between Japan and South Korea, the more difficult a sound relationship between the two countries will become.

Keep distance from South Korea and China

From the time Shinzo Abe took office, Japan has stressed diplomatic activities, attaching particular importance to the relationship with South Korea. Park Guen-hye has pursued a completely opposite stance, openly criticizing Japan and closing its doors. South Korea has slighted Japan and cozied up to China.

I don't believe Japan should make special efforts to approach South Korea. It should instead leave South Korea alone. It is better for Japan to maintain a certain distance in dealing with South Korea. Japan could even afford to break off relations with South Korea without seriously hurting itself. Rather than having half-baked relations with South Korea, it would be better to have nothing to do with them at all.

The main reason for having half-baked relations with South Korea would be a desire to avoid a messy relationship, a desire to maintain a superficially pleasant relationship. Some people do not tell South Korea what South Korea needs to hear. They do not criticize what ought to be criticized. They talk about friendship while avoiding honesty. They just feel the need to keep talking. These people say Japan must have friendly relations with Korea. They do not point out Korea's problems. They just want to make nice. In Japan, such people are everywhere, and they are the people who have spoiled the relationship the two countries should be having.

A long time ago, Fukuzawa Yukichi said in his books *Summary of Civilization* (1875) and *Secession from Asia* (1885) that Japan should sever its ties to bad friends. Fukuzawa focused on the one-dimensional value system that is unique to China and Korea, and he said Japan had developed a world with a multi-dimensional value system. He argued that Japan should modernize by making use of this multi-dimensional value system. To that end, he said, it is better for Japan to shut out the world of China and Korea with their one-dimensional value system. There is little difference from today's world, in terms of the relationships between Japan and China, Japan and Korea.

Countries must get past their many differences, including those related to value systems, and make efforts to get along. It should be pointed out, though, that it is China and South Korea that are responsible for the fact that their relations with Japan today are the worst they have ever been.

Since the beginning of civilian government in South Korea

(1993) and the Jiang Zemin regime in China (1993), these two countries have taken a hard–line anti-Japan stance. Japan is at a loss to know what to do in its relationships with them. In my view, the best thing for Japan would be to keep a certain distance from these countries. Japan should not go out of its way to try to narrow the distance separating itself from them. It can maintain a certain relationship from a certain distance.

I think this would be the best foreign policy for Japan in its relations with China and South Korea in the coming years.

About the Author, Sonfa Oh

Sonfa Oh was born in Jeju Island, South Korea, in 1956 and is a critic in many fields such as current issues, history, and culture, particularly in East Asian countries. She is also a professor in the School of International Relations at Takushoku University in To-kyo. In 1983, she came to Japan and obtained a BA degree from University of Daito Cultural University and a MA degree from the Graduate School of North American Studies at Tokyo Foreign Language University. While studying there, she began writing *Sukato no kaze* [Fluttering Skirts in the Breeze, (Sankou Sha)], in which she compared Japanese and Korean culture, taking into account her own life experiences in the two countries. In 1990 this book became a best-seller in Japan. Since then, she has been a prolific writer and as an opinion leader published more than 50 books, critically evaluating historical and cultural aspects of Japan and the Korean Peninsula, including, *Naze hannichi Kankoku ni mirai wa nai no ka* [Why the Anti-Japan Korean Has no Future] (Shogakukan), *'Hannichi Shinpoku' Kankoku no boso* [Reckless South Korea: Anti-Japan and Pro-North] (Shogakukan), *'Joi no Kankoku kaikoku no Nihon'* [Anti-Foreign Korea and Pro-Foreign Japan] (Bungeishunju). Her books have greatly contributed to mutual understanding between the two regions.

About the Translator, Ichiro Otani

Ichiro Otani, born in 1942, received a BA in economics from the University of California, Berkeley, and an MA in economics from the University of Minnesota. He worked at the International Monetary Fund (IMF) for nearly 35 years and served as head of the IMF office in Beijing, China, for four years beginning in 1999. He retired from the IMF in 2003. Since then he has been an independent international consultant and taught macroeconomic management at Hitotsubashi University. He also taught at international and Japanese universities and has given lectures at many universities in Japan. He has published, a number of research papers on macroeconomics and international finance in English-language academic journals.